"Left Wing" Co[

An Infantile ᑐ

By NIKOLAI LENIN

Martino Fine Books

Eastford, CT

2018

Martino Fine Books
P.O. Box 913,
Eastford, CT 06242 USA

ISBN   978-1-68422-217-9

Copyright 2018
Martino Fine Books

Cover Design Tiziana Matarazzo

Printed in the United States of America On 100% Acid-Free Paper

"Left Wing" Communism

An Infantile Disorder

By NIKOLAI LENIN

LONDON

The Communist Party
of Great Britain

21a Maiden Lane, W.C.2

Contents

Appendix

"Left Wing" Communism:

An Infantile Disorder

By NIKOLAI LENIN

I

In What Sense can we Speak of the International Significance of the Russian Revolution?

DURING the first months after the Russian proletariat had conquered political power (October 25 [November 7], 1917,) it might have seemed that the proletarian revolution in other countries would be very little like ours, because of the tremendous differences between backward Russia and the advanced countries of Western Europe. But we have now considerable experience, of an international scope, which pretty definitely establishes the fact that some fundamental features of our revolution are not local, not peculiarly national, not Russian only, but that they are of international significance. And I say "international significance," not in the broad sense of the word; not some features, but all fundamental and many secondary features are, in the sense of their influence upon other countries, of international significance. Not in the strictest sense of the word—that is, taking it in its essence—or in the sense of the historical inevitability of a repetition, on an international scale, of what we in Russia have gone through; but one must admit some fundamental features of our revolution to be of such international significance. Of course, it would be the greatest mistake to exaggerate this truth and to apply it to more than the fundamental features of our revolution. It would be likewise erroneous not to keep in mind that, after the proletarian revolution in at least one of the advanced countries, things will in all probability take a sharp turn; Russia will cease to be the model, and will become again the backward (in the "Soviet" and Socialist sense) country.

But at this historical moment such is the state of affairs that the Russian example reveals something quite essential to all countries in their near and inevitable future. The advanced workers in every land have long understood it—although in many cases they did not so much understand it as feel it, through the instinct of their revolutionary class. Hence the international "significance" (in the strict sense of the word) of the Soviet power, as well as of the fundamentals of Bolshevik theory and tactics. This the "revolutionary" leaders of the Second International—Kautsky in Germany, Otto Bauer and Friedrich Adler in Austria—failed to understand and, therefore, turned into reactionaries and advocates of the worst kind of opportunism and social treason. The anonymous pamphlet, *The World Revolution,* which appeared in 1919 in Vienna, shows plainly their whole process of thought or, what is more correct, all their appalling imbecility, pedantry, dastardliness and betrayal of working-class interests under the guise of "defending" the idea of "world revolution." Of this pamphlet we shall speak at greater length on some other occasion. Here we shall remark only this: that in the time, now long gone by, when Kautsky was yet a follower of Marx and not the renegade he is to-day, approaching the question as an historian, he fore-saw the possibility of the revolutionary spirit of the Russian proletariat serving as an example for Western Europe. This was in 1902, when Kautsky wrote an article headed "The Slavs and the Revolution," published in the revolutionary organ, *Iskra.* This is what he wrote:—

"At the present time (in contradistinction to the year 1848) it may be assumed that not only have the Slavs entered the ranks of the revolutionary peoples, but that the centre of gravity of revolutionary thought and revolu-tionary action is moving farther and farther to the Slavs. The revolutionary centre is moving from the West to the East. In the first half of the nineteenth century this centre was in France, and sometimes in England. In 1848 Germany entered the ranks of revolutionary nations. The new century is being ushered in by such events as induce us to think that we are confronted by a further removal of the revolutionary centre, namely, to Russia. Russia, which has imbibed so much revolutionary initiative from the West, is now perhaps itself ready to serve as a source of revolutionary energy. The Russian revolutionary movement, which is now bursting into flame, will, perhaps, become the strongest means for the extermination of the senile philistinism and sedate politics which is beginning to spread in our ranks, and will again rekindle the militant spirit and the passionate devotion to our great ideals. Russia has long ceased to be for Western Europe a simple prop for reaction and absolutism. The case now may be said to be reversed. It is Western Europe that is now becoming the mainstay of reaction and absolutism in

Russia. As far as the Czar is concerned, the Russian revolutionists would perhaps have coped with him long ago, had they not been compelled to fight simultaneously his ally, European capital. Let us hope that they will find themselves able this time to settle both enemies, and that the new Holy Alliance' will crash to the ground sooner than its predecessor. But however the present struggle in Russia may end, the blood of the martyrs who have sprung from it, unfortunately in too great numbers, will not have been shed in vain. It will nourish the shoots of the social revolution throughout the civilised world, and make them flourish more quickly. In 1848 the Slavs were that crackling frost which killed the flowers of spring of the awakening peoples; perhaps now they are destined to be that storm which will break through the ice of reaction and will irresistibly bring with it the new, happy spring of the peoples." (Karl Kautsky: "The Slavs and the Revolution," article in *Iskra*, the Russian Social-Democratic revolutionary paper, 1902, No. 18, March 10).

How well did Kautsky write eighteen years ago!

2

One of the Principal Conditions of the Success of the Bolsheviks.

PROBABLY almost everyone can see now that the Bolsheviks could not have maintained themselves in power for two and a-half years, nor even for two and a-half months, without the most stringent, I may say iron, discipline in our party, and without the fullest and unreserved support rendered it by the working class, that is, by that part of it which is sensible, honest, devoted, influential, capable of leading and of inspiring the backward masses with enthusiasm.

The dictatorship of the proletariat is the fiercest and most merciless war of the new class against its more powerful enemy, the bourgeoisie, whose power of resistance increases tenfold after its overthrow, even though overthrown in only one country. The power of the bourgeoisie rests not alone upon international capital, upon its strong international connections, but also upon the force of habit, on the force of small industry of which, unfortunately, there is plenty left, and which daily, hourly, gives birth to capitalism and bourgeoisie, spontaneously and on a large scale. Because of all this, the dictatorship of the proletariat is indispensable. Victory over the bourgeoisie is impossible without a long, persistent, desperate, life and death struggle: a struggle which requires persistence, discipline, firmness, inflexibility and concerted will-power.

I repeat, the experience of the triumphant dictatorship of the proletariat in Russia has furnished an object-lesson to those who are incapable of reasoning or who have had no opportunity to reason on this question. It proves that unqualified centralisation and the strictest discipline of the proletariat are among the principal conditions for the victory over the bourgeoisie. Here people usually stop. They do not inquire sufficiently into the meaning of the dictatorship of the proletariat, and under what conditions it is possible. Would it not be better to accompany the greetings to the Soviet power and the Bolsheviks by a more searching analysis of the reasons why the latter were able to institute a discipline necessary for the revolutionary proletariat?

Bolshevism, as a current of political thought and as a political party, dates back to the year 1903. Only the history of its whole period of existence can explain satisfactorily why it was able to institute and maintain, under most difficult conditions, the iron discipline necessary for the proletarian victory.

And, first of all, the question arises—Upon what rests the discipline of the revolutionary party of the proletariat? How is it controlled? How is it strengthened? First, by the class-consciousness of the proletarian vanguard and by its devotion to the Revolution, by its steadiness, spirit of self-sacrifice, and heroism. Secondly, by its ability to mix with the toiling masses, to become intimate and, to a certain extent if you will, fuse itself with the non-proletarian toilers. Thirdly, by the soundness of the political leadership, carried out by this vanguard, and by its correct political strategy and tactics, based on the idea that the workers from their own experience must convince themselves of the soundness of this political leadership, strategy and tactics. Without all these conditions discipline in a revolutionary party, really capable of being a party of the foremost class whose object is to overthrow the bourgeoisie and transform society, is impossible of realisation. Without these conditions all attempts to create discipline result in empty phrases, in mere contortions. On the other hand, these conditions will not arise suddenly. They are created through long effort and bitter experience. Their creation is facilitated by correct revolutionary theory, which in its turn is not dogmatic, but which forms itself in its finality only through close connection with the practice of the real mass and truly revolutionary movement.

If Bolshevism could successfully, and under the greatest difficulties, achieve in 1917—1920 the strictest centralisation and iron discipline, it was due simply to a series of historical peculiarities of Russia.

On the one hand, Bolshevism came into being in 1903 on the very firm foundation of Marxian theory. And the soundness of this revolutionary theory, and of no other, was proved not only by the experience of all countries during the entire 19th century, but particularly by the experience of the ramblings, vacillations, mistakes and disappointments of revolutionary thought in Russia. For half a century—approximately between the forties and nineties of the preceding century—advanced intellects in Russia, under the yoke of the wildest and most reactionary Czarism, sought eagerly for a correct revolutionary theory, following each and every "last word" in Europe and America with astounding diligence and thoroughness. Russia has attained Marxism, the only revolutionary theory, by dint of fifty years' travail and sacrifice, through the greatest revolutionary heroism, the most incredible energy and devotion in seeking, educating, practical experience, disappointment, checking and comparison with European experience. Thanks to the emigration forced by the Czar, revolutionary Russia, in the second half of the 19th century, came into possession of rich international connections, and of a grasp of the superlative forms and theories of the revolutionary movement abroad, such as no other country had.

On the other hand, having come into existence on this granite theoretical foundation, Bolshevism went through fifteen years (1903—1917) of practical history which, in fertility of experience, had no equal anywhere else in the world. In no other country, during those fifteen years, was there anything approximating to such wide revolutionary experience, such a variety and rapidity of shifting forms in the movement—legal and illegal, peaceful and stormy, open and underground, embracing small circles and large masses, parliamentary and terrorist. In no other country, during so short a period of time, has there been concentrated such a multiplicity of forms, shades and methods of struggle, embracing all classes of modern society. To this it must be added that the struggle maturing with particular rapidity, because of the backwardness of the country and the heavy yoke of Czarism, assimilated eagerly and successfully the latest developments of American and European political experience

3

The Chief Stages in the History of Bolshevism.

1902-1905: *the years of preparation for the Revolution*

THE approach of the great storm is felt everywhere. There is a fermentation and preparation in all classes. Abroad, the emigrant press carries on a theoretical discussion of all questions pertaining to the Revolution. The representatives of the three main political currents, of the three principal classes — liberal-bourgeois, petty-bourgeois democratic (concealed under the guise of "Social Democrats" and "Socialist Revolutionaries") and proletarian-revolutionary—anticipate and prepare the approaching class-struggle in the open by their bitter and obdurate fight on questions of programme and tactics. All the problems which the masses were solving in 1905-1906 and 1917-1920 by force of arms, can and should be traced in their embryonic form in the press of that time. Between these three main currents of thought, there are, of course, plenty of intermediary, transient, dwarfed forms. In other words, in the fight of press, parties, factions, groups, the political doctrines of the classes definitely crystallise themselves; there the classes forge the proper ideo-political weapons for the coming battles.

1905-1907: *the years of revolution*. All classes come out into the open. All questions of programme and tactics are tested by the action of the masses. A strike movement, unknown anywhere else in the world for its extent and acuteness, breaks out. The economic strike gives way to the political strike, which, in its turn, grows into a rising. The relations between the proletariat in the van and the vacillating, unstable peasantry in the rear, are tested practically. In the spontaneous development of the struggle, the Soviet form of organisation is born. The disputes, in these days, on the significance of Soviets, anticipate the great struggle of 1917-1920. The interchange of parliamentary and non-parliamentary forms in the struggle, of the tactics of boycott and the tactics of participation in parliament, of legal and illegal methods, and likewise their interrelation and connection—all this is distinguished by wonderful richness of content. As far as the acquisition by masses and leaders, by classes and parties, of the fundamentals of political science is concerned, one month of this period was equivalent to a whole year of "peaceful," "constitutional" development. Without a general rehearsal in 1905, the victory of the October revolution of 1917 would have been impossible.

The years of reaction (1907–1910). Czarism triumphant. All revolutionary and opposition parties are shattered. Depression, demoralisation, schism, dispersal, renegacy, pornography instead of politics. A strengthening of the drift to philosophic idealism; mysticism, as the outer garb of counter-revolutionary tendencies. At the same time, it is the great defeat which gives the revolutionary parties and the revolutionary class a real and useful lesson, a lesson in historical dialectics, a lesson in intelligent understanding, ability and skill in carrying on the political struggle. Friends are better known in misfortune. Defeated armies learn their lesson well.

Triumphant Czarism is compelled, nevertheless, to push forward the disintegration of what remains of the pre-bourgeois, patriarchal state of Russia. She moves along the path of bourgeois development with remarkable rapidity. Illusions, originating outside of and above all classes, that it was possible for Russia to avoid capitalism, are crushingly shattered. The class-struggle assumes altogether new and more intense forms.

The revolutionary parties must continue their training. Heretofore they learned to attack. Now they understand that they must add to their knowledge of attack a knowledge of how best to retreat. It becomes necessary to understand—and the revolutionary class by its own bitter experience learns to understand—that victory is impossible without a knowledge both of how to attack and of how to retreat correctly. Of all the shattered opposition and revolutionary parties, the Bolsheviks effected the most orderly retreat, with the least damage to their "army." They, more than any other, preserved the nucleus of their party, suffered the fewest splits—in the sense of deep, irremediable splits—felt the least demoralisation, and were in the best position to renew work on a large scale efficiently and energetically. The Bolsheviks only attained this by mercilessly exposing and throwing out the revolutionists of phrases, who did not wish to understand that it was necessary to retreat, that it was obligatory upon them to learn how to work legally in the most reactionary parliaments, in the most reactionary trade-unions, co-operatives, workmen's insurance and similar organisations.

The years of revival (1910–1914). At first the revival was exceedingly slow; after the events in the Lena mines in 1912, somewhat more rapid. Overcoming immense difficulties, the Bolsheviks drove back the Mensheviks, whose rôle as bourgeois agents in the working-class movement was

perfectly understood by the whole bourgeoisie after 1905, and who, therefore, were supported by that class against the Bolsheviks. But the latter
would never have succeeded as they did if they had not pursued the right
tactics of co-ordinating illegal forms of work with obligatory utilisation
of all "legal possibilities." In the most reactionary Duma the Bolsheviks
won the whole labour vote.

The first imperialist world-war (1914–1917). Legal parliamentarism, in the
conditions of an extremely reactionary "parliament," renders most useful
service to the revolutionary party, to the Bolsheviks. Bolshevik deputies go
to penal servitude. In the emigrant press, all shades, all distinctions of social-
imperialism, social-chauvinism, social-patriotism, consistent and inconsistent internationalism, pacifism and the revolutionary negation of pacifist
illusions, find full expression. The learned fools and old women of the
Second International who arrogantly and contemptuously turned up their
noses at the many "factions" in Russian Socialism and the stubbornness with
which they fought one another, were unable, when the war deprived them of
their blessed "legality" in all the advanced countries, to organise anything
even approximating such free (illegal) interchange of views and such free
(illegal) hammering-out of the right views, as did the Russian revolutionists
in Switzerland and other countries. Just because of this inability of theirs,
both the downright social-patriots and the "Kautskians" of all countries
have proved the worst kind of traitors to the proletariat. And if the Bolsheviks were able to attain victory in 1917–1920, one of the principal causes
of this victory was that Bolshevism already, in 1914, had mercilessly unmasked
all the abomination, turpitude and criminality of social-chauvinism and
"Kautskianism" (to which Longuetism in France, the views of the leaders of
the Independent Labour Party and the Fabians in England, and of Turati
in Italy, correspond), while the masses, from their own experience, were
becoming more and more convinced of the soundness of the views of the
Bolsheviks.

The second revolution in Russia (from February to October, 1917). Czarism,
now hoary with age, had created, under the heavy blows of this tormenting-
war, a tremendous destructive power which was now directed against it. In
a few days, Russia was turned into a democratic, bourgeois republic, more
free, considering the state of war, than any other country in the world. The
Government was beginning to be formed by the leaders of the Opposition
and Revolutionary parties, just after the manner of the most "strictly parlia-

mentary" republics. The fact that a man had been a leader of the opposition, though in the most reactionary parliament imaginable, aided him in his subsequent career in the Revolution.

The Mensheviks and the "Socialist Revolutionaries" mastered, in a few weeks, all the tricks and manners, arguments and sophistries of the European heroes of the Second International, of the ministerialists and other opportunist worthies. What we now read of Scheideman and Noske, Kautsky and Crispien, Renner and Austerlitz, Otto Bauer and Fritz Adler, Turati and Longuet, of the Fabians and the leaders of the Independent Labour Party in England—all this seems to us, and, in reality, is, a dreary repetition, a paraphrase of an old, familiar song. The Mensheviks have long ago sung it to us. History has played a joke on us and made the opportunists of a backward country anticipate the opportunists of a great many advanced countries.

That all the heroes of the Second International suffered bankruptcy and disgraced themselves on the question of the rôle and significance of the Soviets and Soviet power; that the leaders of three very important parties which have now left the Second International (namely, the German Independent Social Democratic Party, the French Longuetists and the British Independent Labour Party) have especially "vividly" disgraced themselves on this question; that they have all proved slaves to the prejudices of petty-bourgeois democracy (quite in the spirit of the petty-bourgeois of 1848 who called themselves "social democrats")—all this conveys to us nothing new. We have already seen all of it in the example of the Mensheviks. History has played off this joke: in Russia, in 1905, Soviets were born: in February-October, 1917, they were tampered with by the Mensheviks, who went bankrupt because of their inability to understand the rôle and significance of the Soviets, and, now that the idea of Soviets has come to life the world over, spreading itself with tremendous rapidity among the proletariat of all countries, the old heroes of the Second International are also everywhere going bankrupt, because, like our Mensheviks, they are unable to understand the true rôle and significance of Soviets. Experience has shown that, on some very essential points in the proletarian revolution, all countries will inevitably have to repeat Russia's experience.

The successful struggle against what was in reality the parliamentary bourgeois republic, and against the Mensheviks, was begun by the Bolsheviks very cautiously, and, contrary to the view often met with in Europe and America, it was not at all without careful preparation. At the outset of the period indicated, we did *not* call for the overthrow of the government, but explained the impossibility of overthrowing it without a preliminary change in the personnel and disposition of the Soviets. We did not proclaim a boycott of the bourgeois parliament, of the Constitutent Assembly, but said —after the April, 1917, conference of our party officially, in the name of the organisation—that a bourgeois republic with a Constituent Assembly is better than one without, but that a "workmen's and peasants'" Soviet republic is better than any bourgeois democratic, parliamentary, republic. Without such a careful, substantial, cautious and prolonged preparation, we could not have obtained victory in October, 1917, neither could we have maintained it.

B

4

Who were the Enemies in the Working-class Movement in the Struggle against whom Bolshevism Grew, Gained Strength and became Hardened?

FIRST of all, and principally, in the struggle against opportunism, which, in 1914, grew definitely into social chauvinism, and finally deserted to the bourgeoisie against the proletariat. This was naturally the chief enemy of Bolshevism within the movement of the working class, and this remains the chief enemy also on an international scale. This enemy claimed, and claims, most of the attention of the Bolsheviks, whose work in this sphere is already well known abroad.

Something else, however, must be said of the other enemy of Bolshevism in the working-class movement. It is not sufficiently known abroad that Bolshevism grew up, formed, and hardened itself in long years of struggle against *petty-bourgeois revolutionism*, which resembles, or borrows something from, anarchism. It differs in one respect or another, in all essentials, from the conditions and requirements of a consistent proletarian class-struggle. For Marxians it is well-established theoretically—and the experience of all European revolutions and revolutionary movements fully confirms—that the small owner (the social type which in many European countries is very numerous and widespread), who, under capitalism, is constantly oppressed and suffering, and whose conditions of life often take a sharp and rapid turn for the worse, moves easily when faced with ruin to extreme revolutionism, but is incapable of displaying consistency, organisation, discipline and firmness. The petty-bourgeois, "gone mad" from the horrors of capitalism, is a social phenomenon which, like anarchism, is characteristic of all capitalist countries. The weakness of such revolutionism, its futility, its liability swiftly to transform itself into obedience, apathy, phantasy and even into a "mad" infatuation with some bourgeois "fashionable" tendency—all this is a matter of common knowledge. But a mere recognition in the abstract, a theoretical recognition of these truths, does not at all free revolutionary parties from old mistakes, which always appear unexpectedly in a somewhat new form, in new trappings, in more or less original surroundings.

Anarchism was often a kind of punishment for the opportunist sins of the working-class movement. Anarchism and opportunism were two deformities, one complementary to the other. It is partly due to Bolshevism that, notwithstanding the fact that the population of Russia, in comparison with European countries, is largely of a petty-bourgeois make-up, anarchism exercised a comparatively insignificant influence during the revolutions of 1905–1917; for Bolshevism has always carried on a merciless and uncompromising fight against opportunism. I say, it is *partly* due to Bolshevism, for a still greater part in weakening the influence of anarchism in Russia was played by the fact that it had the opportunity to flourish in full bloom in the seventies of the nineteenth century, and to reveal completely its uselessness as a guiding theory of the revolutionary class.

Bolshevism, at its inception in 1903, was imbued with the tradition of merciless struggle with petty-bourgeois, semi-anarchist and dilettante-anarchist revolutionism. This tradition always obtained in the revolutionary social democracy, and gained special strength in Russia in 1900–1903, when the foundations were being laid for a mass party of the revolutionary proletariat. Bolshevism continued the fight with the party which, more than any other, expressed tendencies of a petty-bourgeois revolutionism, namely, with the "Socialist-Revolutionaries." This fight was conducted on three main points. First, this party, rejecting Marxism, stubbornly refused to understand (it would be more correct to say that it could not understand) the necessity of a strictly objective estimate of all the class forces and their interrelation in every political action. Secondly, in its individual terrorism and attempts at assassination, this party saw its peculiar claim to "revolutionism" and "leftness"—a thing which we Marxians rejected. It is, of course, self-evident that we rejected individual terror only from considerations of expediency; for those who would "on principle" condemn the terror of the great French Revolution, or terror generally, on the part of a victorious revolutionary party, besieged by the bourgeoisie of the whole world, had been scorned and ridiculed by Plekhanov in 1900–1903, when he was a Marxist and revolutionary. Thirdly, the "Socialist-Revolutionaries" thought it "leftness" to giggle at the comparatively insignificant sins of the German Social Democrats, while they themselves imitated the extreme opportunists of that party, as, for example, on the question of the dictatorship of the proletariat or the agrarian question.

History, by the way, has now on a large, universal scale, confirmed the opinion always advocated by us, that the revolutionary German Social Democracy (note the fact that Plekhanov, even in 1900–1903, demanded the expulsion of Bernstein from the Party, and the Bolsheviks, always continuing this tradition, in 1913 exposed the whole baseness, knavery and treachery of Legien) was the *nearest* approximation to that party which is necessary to the revolutionary proletariat to enable it to attain victory. Now, in 1920, after the ignominious failures, bankruptcy and crises during the war and the first years after, it can be seen plainly that of all the Western parties it was the German revolutionary social democracy which gave the best leaders, restored itself, healed its wounds and gained new strength before all the others. This may be seen in the example of both the party of the Spartacists and the left, proletarian, wing of the "Independent Social-Democratic Party of Germany," which carries on an incessant fight with the opportunism and characterlessness of the Kautskys, Hilferdings, Ledebours, and Crispiens.

If we now take a general view of the historical period now completed—namely, from the Paris Commune to the first Socialist Soviet Republic—we shall see in very clear perspective the whole attitude of Marxism towards anarchism. Marxism was right after all, and, if the anarchists rightly pointed to the opportunism in the conception of the State, a conception predominant in most of the Socialist Parties, it was not the fault of Marxism. First, this opportunism was due to misrepresentation and even downright concealment of Marx's views on the conception of the State. (In my book, *The State and Revolution,* I called attention to the fact that for thirty-six years, 1875 to 1911, Bebel kept unpublished a letter by Engels which very vividly, pointedly, directly and clearly denounced the opportunism of the popular social-democratic conception of the State.) Secondly, it was the truly Marxian tendencies in the European and American Socialist Parties that were responsible for modifying these opportunist conceptions by accepting Soviet power and recognising its advantages over bourgeois parliamentary democracy.

There were two instances in which Bolshevism carried on an especially arduous struggle against a "turn to the left" within its own party; one was in 1908, on the question whether or not to participate in the most reactionary "parliament" and in the legal workers' societies, bound by the most reactionary laws and regulations; and again in 1918 (the Brest Treaty) on the question of whether any "compromise" is admissible.

In 1908 the "left" Bolsheviks were expelled from the Party for their stubborn refusal to understand the necessity of participating in the most reactionary "parliament." The "left," among whom there were some very excellent revolutionaries, who subsequently became, and continue to be, prominent members of the Communist Party, sought vindication in the policy of the boycott of the Duma in 1905, a particularly successful experience. When the Czar, in August, 1905, proclaimed the convocation of a consultative "parliament," the Bolsheviks came out with a declaration of boycott, in contradistinction to all the opposition parties and the Mensheviks. The October Revolution of 1905 actually swept away that "parliament." At that time the boycott proved right, not because non-participation in reactionary parliaments is right, but because when we studied the objective situation we saw that it led to the rapid transformation of mass strikes into political, then into revolutionary strikes, and after that, into a rising. Besides, the struggle then was revolving around the question whether to leave it in the hands of the Czar to convoke the first representative assembly or to attempt to take the convocation of the assembly out of the hands of the old government. In so far as there was not, and could not be, the certainty that we were faced with an objective situation developing in a similar direction and at a similar pace the boycott ceased to be sound policy.

The Bolshevik boycott of "parliament" in 1905 enriched the revolutionary proletariat with highly valuable political experience, having shown that, by combining legal with illegal, parliamentary with non-parliamentary, forms of struggle, it may become necessary, and even essential, sometimes to be able to reject parliamentary forms. But to transfer this experience blindly, imitatively, uncritically, into different surroundings and different conditions is the greatest possible mistake. A small error easily corrected* was the boycott of the Duma by the Bolsheviks in 1906. Very serious and not at all easy to correct was the mistake of boycotting the Duma in 1907, 1908 and after, when a rapid rising of the revolutionary wave, resulting in an armed insurrection, could not be expected, and when, on the other hand, all the historical circumstances now strengthened by the bourgeois monarchy dictated the necessity of combining legal with illegal forms of work. Now, when we look back upon the complete historical period, whose connection with the following periods has fully revealed itself, it becomes particularly clear that the Bolsheviks would not have been able to preserve, certainly not to strengthen, develop and reinforce the stable nucleus of the revolutionary

* What is said of individuals may be said, with necessary modifications, of politics and parties. The wise man is not he who makes no mistakes. There are not, and cannot be, such men. He is wise who makes slight mistakes and who is able to correct them easily and quickly

party of the proletariat in 1908–1914 if they had not succeeded in maintaining, by a rigorous struggle, that it is obligatory to participate in the most reactionary parliament and in many other organisations bound by the most reactionary laws (Workmen's Insurance Societies, etc.).

In 1918 things did not go so far as to bring about a "split." The "left" Communists formed a separate group or "faction" within our party, but it was short-lived. The same year, the most prominent representatives of "left Communism," as, for example, Comrades Radek and Bukharin, openly admitted their mistake. It seemed to them that the Brest Treaty was, on principle, inadmissible, and a compromise with imperialists dangerous to the party of the revolutionary proletariat. In truth it was a compromise with imperialists, but it was a compromise which, in the given surroundings, was *imperative.*

To-day, when I hear criticism, for instance by the Socialist Revolutionaries, of our tactics in signing the Brest Treaty, or when I hear the remark of Comrade Lansbury, made by him in a conversation with me: "Our English trade unionists say that they should be allowed compromises, since Bolshevism allowed itself compromises," I usually reply first of all by way of a simple and "popular" comparison:

Imagine that your automobile is held up by armed bandits. You hand them over your money, passport, revolver, the machine. In return you are spared the pleasant company of the bandits. The compromise is plainly there. "Do, ut des" (I "give" you money, arms, the automobile, in order that you "give" me the possibility of going in peace). But one can hardly find a sane man who would pronounce such a compromise "inadmissible on principle," or would proclaim the compromiser an accomplice of the bandits—even though the bandits, having got into the automobile, used it and the firearms for new robberies, as was the case with me. Our compromise with the bandits of German imperialism was such a compromise.

But, when the Mensheviks and Socialist Revolutionaries in Russia, the Scheidemanns (and to a great extent the Kautskians) in Germany, Otto Bauer and Friedrich Adler (let alone the Messrs. Renner and Co.) in Austria, the Renaudels, Longuets and Co. in France, the "Independents" and the "Labourites" and the Fabians in England, effected in 1914–1918, and in 1918–1920, compromises with the bandits of their own bourgeoisie, and sometimes with those of the bourgeoisie of the "Allies," against the revolu-

tionary proletariat of their country, that is where these worthies were guilty
of aiding and abetting.

The conclusion is clear: To reject compromises on "principle," to reject
every admissibility of compromises generally, no matter of what kind, is a
a piece of childishness hard even to take seriously. He who wishes to be
useful to the revolutionary proletariat must be able to sift the concrete cases
of such compromises which are inadmissible, which stand for opportunism
and treachery, and to direct all the force of his criticism against these concrete compromises, mercilessly exposing them, fighting them to a finish, and
not allowing "experienced Socialists" and parliamentary Jesuits to dodge
and shirk responsibilities by resorting to discussions of "compromises
generally." The "leaders" of the British trade unions, as well as of the Fabian
Society and the "Independent" Labour Party, use just this method of dodging
responsibility for the betrayal they committed. Theirs was a compromise
which indicated the worst kind of opportunism, treason and betrayal.

There are compromises and compromises. It is necessary to be able to
analyse the situation and the concrete facts of each compromise or of each
species of compromise. It is necessary to learn to distinguish the man who
gave the bandits money and arms in order to lessen the evil caused by this
gentry and to facilitate the business of capturing and shooting them, from the
man who gives to bandits money and arms in order to share the booty. In
politics it is not always so easy to make distinctions as in this childishly
simple little example. But whoever took it into his head that he could contrive for the workers a formula which would give beforehand ready solutions
of all cases, or who would assert that in the political experience of the revolutionary proletariat there will be no difficulties, no intricate problems to solve,
would be merely a charlatan. To leave no room for misunderstandings, I
shall attempt to outline very briefly a few fundamental rules for the analysis
of concrete compromises.

The party which compromised with German imperialism by signing the
Brest Treaty had been evolving internationalism in deed since the end of
1914. It did not fear to proclaim the defeat of the Czarist monarchy and to
repudiate the "defence of the Fatherland" in a war between two imperialist
plunderers. The members of this party in the Duma preferred the road to
penal servitude in Siberia rather than the road leading to ministerial port-
folios in bourgeois governments. The revolution, which overthrew Czarism
and established the democratic republic, subjected the party to a new and

tremendous test; the party rejected all temporising with "its own" imperi-alists, but prepared their overthrow and did overthrow them. Having taken over the political power, not the smallest fragment was left, either of the property of the landlords or of the capitalists. After publishing and repudi-ating the secret treaties of the imperialists, this party proposed peace to *all* the peoples, and yielded to the Brest plunderers only after the Anglo-French imperialists had caused our peace proposals to miscarry, and after the Bolsheviks had done everything humanly possible to hasten the revolution in Germany and other countries. That such a compromise made by such a party in such a situation was absolutely correct, becomes clearer and more self-evident to everyone from day to day.

The Mensheviks and the Socialist-Revolutionaries in Russia (like the leaders of the Second International in 1914–20 the world over) began their betrayal by justifying the "defence of the Fatherland," that is, the defence of their marauding bourgeoisie. They continued their betrayal by entering into a coalition with the bourgeoisie against the revolutionary proletariat of their country. Their bloc, first with Kerensky and the Cadets (Constitutional Democrats), then with Koltchak and Denikin in Russia, like the bloc of their confrères abroad with the bourgeoisie of their respective countries, was the bridge which led them to alliance with the bourgeoisie against the proletariat. Their compromise with the bandits of imperialism consisted from beginning to end in their willing participation in imperialist robbery.

5

"Left" Communism in Germany : Leaders-Party-Classes The Masses.

THE German Communists, of whom we shall now speak, call themselves not "left," but, if I am not mistaken, the "opposition on principle." That they fully come under the symptoms of the "infantile disorder of leftness" will be seen from what follows.

A small pamphlet headed, "The Split in the Communist Party of Germany" (the Spartacist Union) issued by "the local groups in Frankfurt-am-Maine," sets forth pointedly, concisely, clearly and briefly the substance of the views of the opposition. A few quotations will suffice to acquaint the reader with the essential points:

"The Communist Party is a party of the most decisive class struggle. . . ."

"Politically, this transition period (between capitalism and Socialism) is the period of the proletarian dictatorship. . . ."

"The question arises: Who should be the wielder of this dictatorship; *the Communist Party or the proletarian class. . . . ?*"

"*On principle,* should we strive towards the dictatorship of the Communist Party or the dictatorship of the proletariat? ! ! " (Italics in the original).

Further, the E.C. of the Communist Party of Germany is accused by the author of the pamphlet of seeking a way to a coalition with the Independent Socialist Party of Germany; that "the question of accepting, as a matter of principle all political means of struggle" including parliamentarism, has been put to the forefront by the E.C. only for the purpose of concealing its main and real intention, coalition with the Independents. And the pamphlet goes on :

"The Opposition has selected a different road. It is of the opinion that the question of the supremacy of the Communist Party and of its dictatorship is only a question of tactics. At any rate, the supremacy of the Communist Party is the last form of any party supremacy. On principle, we must strive towards the dictatorship of the proletariat, and all the party measures, its organisation, methods of struggle, its strategy and tactics must be planned to fit accordingly. Therefore, every compromise with other parties must be rejected. There must be no turning back to the already outworn historical and political forms of the parliamentary struggle, no policy of manœuvring and temporising." "The specifically proletarian methods of the revolutionary struggle must be strongly emphasised. In order to embrace the greatest mass of the proletariat which is to carry on the revolutionary fight under the leadership of the Communist Party, there must be created new forms of organisation upon the broadest foundations and within the widest limits. The gathering place for all revolutionary elements is the *Workers' Union,* formed on the basis of the shop committee. Here all the workers who followed the slogan of "Leave the trade unions" must gather and unite; here the militant proletariat draws itself up in the thickest ranks. The acceptance of the class struggle, the Soviet system and the dictatorship, is sufficient for admittance. All further political training of the struggling masses, and the political orientation of the struggle, is the task of the Communist Party, standing outside the Workers' Union. . . ."

"Two Communist Parties are consequently arrayed, one against the other. One party of the leaders, a party which strives to organise the revolutionary struggle and direct it from above, resorting to compromises and parliamentarism in order to create a situation which would enable it to enter a coalition government, in whose hands should rest the dictatorship. The other, a mass party which relies upon the impetus of the revolutionary struggle from below, conscious of and applying but one method in the fight, that method leading clearly to the goal; rejecting all parliamentary and opportunist procedure. Unconditional overthrow of the bourgeoisie, in order to establish the proletarian class dictatorship for the realisation of Socialism, that is the only possible method. . . ."

"There the dictatorship of the leaders, here the dictatorship of the mass—such is our slogan."

These are the essential points characterising the views of the Opposition in the German Communist Party.

Any Bolshevik who has consciously participated in, or watched closely, the developments of his party since 1903 will at once say, after reading these arguments, "What old and well-known rubbish! What ' left ' childishness!"

But let us look at these arguments a little more closely. The very question, "Dictatorship of the party *or* dictatorship of the class, dictatorship of the leaders *or* dictatorship of the masses" bears witness to an amazing and hopeless confusion of mind. People bend every effort to elaborate something extraordinary, and in their zeal to be intellectual they become ridiculous. It is common knowledge that the masses are divided into classes; that to contrast masses with classes is possible only when we contrast the largest general majority, undivided in respect of its position in the social scale with categories occupying a definite position in the social scale; that the classes are usually and in most cases led by political parties, at least in modern civilised countries; that political parties, as a general rule, are led by more or less stable groups of the more influential, authoritative, experienced members, elected to the most responsible positions, and called leaders. All this is elementary. It is simple and plain. Why then all this rigmarole, this new Volapuk?

On the one hand, men who were confronted with great difficulties, when the rapid alternation between legal to illegal existence interrupted the usual normal, simple relations between leaders, parties and classes, apparently lost their head. In Germany, as in other European countries, people had become much used to over legality, to the free and normal election of their "leaders" at the regular party conventions, to convenient methods of testing the class composition of the party through parliamentary elections, meetings, the Press and the temper of the members of the trade and other unions, etc. When, in face of the stormy advance of the revolution and the spread of civil war, it became necessary to shift quickly from legal to illegal positions, to co-ordinate them, to resort to "inconvenient" and "undemocratic" methods of picking out or constituting or preserving "groups of leaders", people lost their heads and began inventing all sorts of supernatural nonsense. Probably some members of the Dutch Communist Party who had the misfortune to be born in a small country, into traditions and conditions of particularly privileged and stable legality, who have not known at all what it means to shift from a legal to an illegal position, got themselves entangled and contributed to this muddle.

On the other hand, one notices the superficial and incoherent use of the now "fashionable" terms "masses" and "leaders." People have heard much and have conned by rote all the frivolous attacks on "leaders"—contrasting them with the "masses"—but failed to grasp the application and the inner meaning of these words.

The parting of the ways of "leaders" and "masses" showed itself with peculiar clarity and sharpness in all countries at the end of and after the imperialist war. The principal cause of this phenomenon was many times explained by Marx and Engels in 1852–92 by the example of England. The dominant position of England created in the "masses" a labour aristocracy, petty bourgeois and opportunist. The leaders of this labour aristocracy constantly deserted to the bourgeoisie, and were directly or indirectly in its pay. Marx, to his honour, roused the hatred of these wretches by openly branding them as traitors. The newest (20th century) imperialism has created a monopolist, privileged position for a few advanced countries, and this brought to the surface everywhere in the Second International a certain type of leader-traitors, opportunists, social-chauvinists, who look after the interests of their particular group in the labour aristocracy. This caused the opportunist parties to break away from the "masses," that is, from the greatest mass of the toilers, from the majority of the working-class, from the lowest paid workers. The victory of the working-class is impossible unless this evil is fought, unless the opportunist, social-traitor leaders are exposed, disgraced and expelled. The Third International pursues this policy.

To twist the subject so as to draw comparisons between dictatorship of the mass generally and dictatorship of the leaders is a laughable absurdity and piece of foolishness. It is especially comical that, instead of old leaders who have a common-sense viewpoint on ordinary matters, new leaders are put forth (concealed under the slogan of "down with leaders") who prattle supernatural nonsense and spread confusion. Such are Laufenberg, Wolfheim, Horner, Karl Schroeder, Friedrich Wendell, and Karl Erler in Germany.*

The attempt by the latter to make the question "more profound," and to proclaim that political parties altogether are unnecessary and "bourgeois," reaches such a Herculean pitch of absurdity that one is perplexed how to describe it in speech. Verily it may be said, that a small mistake persisted in, learnedly demonstrated, and "carried to its logical conclusion," will grow into a monstrosity.

---

* See the *Commun. Arb. Zeitung,* Hamburg, January 7, 1920, No. 32; "Ausflösung der Partei" (The Dissolution of the Party), by Karl Erler: "The working-class cannot destroy the bourgeois state without destroying the bourgeois democracy, and it cannot destroy bourgeois democracy without the abolition of the party." ("Die Arbeiter Klasse kann den burgerlichen Staat nicht zertrummern ohne Vernichtung der burgerlichen Democratie, u. sie kann die burgerliche Democratie nicht vernichten ohne die Zertrummerung der Parteien.")

The more muddle-headed among the syndicalists and anarchists of the Latin countries may enjoy a certain self satisfaction: serious Germans, who evidently consider themselves Marxists (K. Erler and K. Horner in their articles in the above-mentioned papers particularly solidly maintain that they are solid Marxists, all the more ludicrously revealing their ignorance of the A B C of Marxism by talking incredible nonsense) talk themselves into a point of view altogether inappropriate. Acceptance of Marxism does not save one from mistakes, and the Russians especially know this well, because, in our country, Marxism was particularly frequently " in fashion."

The negation of party and party discipline—that is the result of the arguments of the Opposition. And this is equivalent to disarming the proletariat in favour of the bourgeoisie. It is akin to that petty-bourgeois looseness, instability, incapacity for steady, unified, and harmonious action, which, if given encouragement, must bring to nought every proletarian revolutionary movement. To reject party, from the view-point of Communism, means to leap from the eve of the capitalist overthrow (in Germany), not to the initial or middle stages of Communism, but to its highest phase. We in Russia, in the third year after the overthrow of the bourgeoisie, are going through the first steps in the transition from capitalism to Socialism, that is to say, the lowest stage of Communism. Classes remain, and will remain for years, everywhere after the proletarian conquest of power. Perhaps in England, where there is no peasantry, the period will be shorter, but even there small owners, holders of property exist. To abolish classes means not only to get rid of landlords and capitalists—that we have accomplished with comparative ease—it means also to get rid of the small commodity producers, and they cannot be eliminated or suppressed. There must be an understanding with them, they can and should be regenerated, re-trained; but this requires a long, gradual, careful organisation. They surround the proletariat on every side with a petty bourgeois atmosphere, impregnating the proletariat with it, corrupting and demoralising the proletariat, causing it to relapse into petty-bourgeois lack of character, disintegration, individualism, and alternation between moods of exaltation and dejection. To oppose this, it is necessary to have the strictest centralisation and discipline within the political party of the proletariat. It is necessary, in order to carry on the *organising* activities of the proletariat (and this is its principal rôle) correctly, successfully, victoriously. The dictatorship of the proletariat is a resolute persistent struggle, sanguinary and bloodless, violent and peaceful, military and economic, educational and administrative, against the forces and traditions of the old society. The force of habit of the millions and tens of millions is a formidable force. Without an iron party hardened in fight, without a party possessing the confidence of all that is honest in the given class, without a party capable of observing the disposition of the masses and of influencing it successfully to conduct such a struggle is impossible. To defeat the great, centralised bourgeoisie is a thousand times easier than to "defeat" millions and millions of small owners who in their daily, imperceptible, inconspicuous but demoralising activities achieve the very results desired by the bourgeoisie, and restore the bourgeoisie. Whoever in the least weakens the iron discipline of the party of the proletariat (especially during its dictatorship), aids in reality the bourgeoisie against the proletariat.

Beside the question of leaders, of party, of class, and of the masses, it is necessary to raise the question of the "reactionary" Trade Unions. But first I shall take the liberty of making a few concluding remarks based upon the experience of our party. There, we always heard attacks upon the "dictatorship of the leaders." I remember having heard such attacks for the first time in 1895 when formally there was as yet no party, but only a central group, which began to form itself in Petersburg, and which was to assume the leadership over the district groups. At the ninth conference of our party (April, 1920) there was a small opposition, which also spoke against the "dictatorship of the leaders," of "oligarchy," etc. There is, therefore, nothing wonderful, nothing new, nothing terrible in the "infantile disorder" of "Left Communism," in Germany. It is an affliction which passes by without injury to the organism, which, in fact, even strengthens it afterwards. On the other hand, the rapid shifting from legal to illegal work which made it especially necessary to "hide" the movements of the general staff, that is to say, the leaders, sometimes gave rise to dangerous situations. The worst case was in 1912, when an agent-provocateur, Malinovsky, got into the Central Committee of the Bolsheviks. He betrayed scores of the best and most devoted comrades, causing their imprisonment and hastening their death. That he did not cause more mischief was due to the efficient co-ordination between the legal and illegal forms of our activities. Malinovsky, as a member of the Central Committee of the Party and a deputy in the Duma, was forced, in order to gain our confidence, to aid us in establishing daily papers, which even under the Czar knew how to carry on the fight openly against the opportunism of the Mensheviks, and to preach the fundamentals of Bolshevism in properly disguised forms. With one hand, Malinovsky sent to jail and to death scores upon scores of the most active Bolsheviks, while with the other he was compelled to aid in the training of scores and scores of thousands of new adherents through the medium of the legal Press. It will not harm those of our German comrades (as well as the English, French, Italian and American), who are confronted with the problem of how to carry on revolutionary work inside the reactionary trade unions, to consider this fact seriously.*

* Malinovsky was a prisoner of war in Germany. When he returned to Soviet Russia, he was instantly arrested, tried and shot by our working men. The Mensheviks attacked

In many countries, and particularly in the most advanced, the bourgeoisie is undoubtedly sending, and will continue to send, agents-provocateurs into the Communist Parties. One method of struggle against this peril is a skilful co-ordination of legal and illegal work.

us acrimoniously for our mistake in making an agent-provocateur a member of the Centra Committee of our party. But when, under Kerensky, we demanded the arrest of Rodzianko, the Speaker of the Duma, in order to try him for his having known, even before the war, that Malinovsky was an agent-provocateur, and for his failure to inform the Labour group in the Duma and the workers of this fact, the Mensheviks and Socialist-Revolutionaries who were in Kerensky's cabinet did not support our demand, Rodzianko remained at large, and then went off freely to Denikin.

6

Should Revolutionaries Work in Reactionary Trade Unions?

THE German "Left" consider the reply to this question to be decidedly in the negative so far as they are concerned. According to their opinion, mere declamations and angry ejaculations (as done by K. Horner in a particularly "solid" and stupid manner) against "reactionary" and "counter-revolutionary" Trade Unions are sufficient to prove that it is not only useless but also not permissible for revolutionaries and Communists to work in the yellow, social-chauvinist, temporising and conservative organisations of the type of the Legien Unions. But, however strongly the German "Left" may be convinced of the revolutionary nature of such tactics, these are in reality fundamentally wrong, and contain nothing but empty phrases.

In order to explain this, I shall begin with our own experience, in so far as it coincides with the general scheme of the present article, the aim of which is to apply to Western Europe everything that is of general significance in the history and the present tactics of Bolshevism.

The relation between leaders, party, class, masses, and at the same time the relation of the proletarian dictatorship and its Party to the Trade Unions, present themselves to us in the following concrete form. The dictatorship of the proletariat is carried out by the proletariat organised in Soviets, which is led by the Communist Party (Bolsheviks), which, according to the data of the last party Conference, in April, 1920, has 611,000 members. The number of members varied greatly both before and after the October Revolution, and was considerably less even in 1918 and 1919. We are afraid of too wide a growth of the Party, as place-seekers and adventurers, who deserve only to be shot, do their utmost to get into the ruling Party. The last time we opened wide the doors of the Party for workmen and peasants only was in the days (winter, 1919) when Yudenitch was a few versts from Petrograd, and Denikin was in Orel (about 350 versts from Moscow); that is, when the Soviet Republic was in mortal danger, and when the adventurers, place-seekers, charlatans and unreliable persons generally could in no way rely upon making a profitable career (in fact could sooner expect the gallows and torture) by joining the Communists. The Party, which convenes annual Conferences (the last on the basis of one delegate for each 1,000 members), is directed by a Central Committee of 19, elected at the Conference; while the current work in Moscow has to be done by still smaller boards, viz., the so-called "Org-bureau" (Organising Bureau) and "Politbureau" (Political Bureau), which are elected at the plenary sessions of the Central Committee, five members of the C.C. for each Bureau. This, then, looks like a real "oligarchy." Not a single important political or organising question is decided by any State institution in our Republic without the guiding instructions of the C.C. of the Party.

In carrying on its work, the Party rests directly on the Trade Unions, which, at present, according to the data of the last Conference (April, 1920), comprise over 4,000,000 members, who are formally non-party. In reality, all the controlling bodies of by far the greater number of unions, and primarily, of course, of the All-Russian Centre or Bureau (A.R.C.T.U. All-Russian Central Council of Trade Unions) consist of Communists, who carry out all the directions of the Party. Thus is obtained, on the whole, a formally non-Communist, flexible, comparatively extensive and very powerful pro-letarian apparatus, by means of which the Party is closely connected with the class and the masses, and by means of which, under the guidance of the Party, class dictatorship is realised. Without the closest connection with the Trade Unions, without their hearty support and self-sacrificing work, not only in economic but also in military organisation, it would have been, of course, impossible to govern the country and to maintain the dictatorship for two and a-half years, or even for two and a-half months. It is clear that, in practice, this closest connection means very complicated and varied work in the form of propaganda, agitation, conferences—held often and at the right time, not only with the leading but also with the generally influential Trade Union workers; it also means a determined struggle against the Men-sheviks, who still have a certain, though quite a small, number of adherents, whom they teach various counter-revolutionary tricks, such as lending moral support to the cause of (bourgeois) democracy, preaching the "independence" of Trade Unions (independence of the proletarian State!) and even sabotage of proletarian discipline, etc., etc.

The connection with the "masses" through Trade Unions we admit to be insufficient. Practice in the course of the revolution has given rise to non-party workers' and peasants' Conferences, and we endeavour by every means to support, develop, and extend such institutions in order to maintain a close contact with the disposition and state of mind of the masses, to respond to their inquiries, to push forward the best of their workers to take positions

C

in State institutions, etc., etc. In one of the last decrees concerning the trans-formation of the People's Commissariat for State Control into the "Work-men's and Peasants' Inspection," non-party Conferences of this kind are given the right to elect members to the State Control for various sorts of State inspections.

Then, of course, all the work of the Party is done through the Soviets, which unite the labouring masses irrespective of the difference of their trade or profession. The County (Uyezd) Congresses of Soviets are a democratic institution such as has never yet been seen in the most advanced bourgeois republics. Through these Congresses, whose proceedings are followed by the Party with very careful attention, as well as through the constant dele-gation of class-conscious workmen to occupy various positions in the country-side, the city fulfils its function of leading the peasantry. Thus is carried out the dictatorship of the proletariat, and the systematic struggle against the rich, exploiting, and speculating peasantry.

Such is the general mechanism of the proletarian State considered from "above," from the point of view of practice in realisation of the dictatorship. It is hoped that the reader will understand why, to a Russian Bolshevik well acquainted with this mechanism and having watched its growth out of small underground circles during twenty-five years, all talk of "from above" or "from below," "the dictatorship of leaders" or "the dictatorship of the masses" cannot but appear as childish nonsense. It is something like discussing whether the left leg or the right arm is more useful to man.

Not less laughable and childishly nonsensical appears to us the important, learned and horribly revolutionary disquisitions of the German "Left" as to why Communists cannot and should not work in reactionary Trade Unions; why it is permissible to refuse such work; why it is necessary to leave the craft unions and to create in their stead quite new and quite pure "workmen's unions" invented by exceedingly nice (and, for the most part, probably very youthful) Communists, etc., etc.

Capitalism inevitably leaves, as an inheritance to Socialism, on the one hand, old professional and craft differences created among the workers in the course of centuries; and on the other, Trade Unions, which only, very slowly and in the course of years, can and will develop into broader industrial rather than craft organisations (embracing whole industries and not merely crafts, trades and professions). These industrial unions will, in their turn, lead to the abolition of division of labour between people, to the education, training and preparation of workers, who will be able to do *everything*. Communism is moving in this direction; it must move and will arrive at that goal but only after a great many years. To attempt in practice to-day, to precipitate development of this characteristic of a thoroughly developed, stable and completely matured Communism would be like trying to teach a four-year-old child higher mathematics.

We can and must begin to build up Socialism, not with the fantastic human material created by our imagination, but out of the material left to us by capitalism. This, no doubt, is very "difficult," but every other way of tackling the problem is not serious enough to even discuss.

Trade Unions marked a gigantic step forward of the working class at the beginning of capitalist development, as a transition from the disintegration and helplessness of the workers to the beginnings of class organisations. When the proletarian revolutionary party (which does not deserve the name until it learns to connect leaders-class-masses into one single indissoluble whole), when this last, *highest,* form of proletarian class-organisation began to grow up, the Trade Unions unavoidably revealed some reactionary traits, a certain craft limitation, a certain tendency to non-political action, a certain conservatism, etc., etc. But the development of the proletariat did not and could not, anywhere in the world, proceed by any other road than that of Trade Unions, with their mutual activity with the working-class party. The seizing of political power by the proletariat, as a class, is a gigantic step forward; and it is incumbent upon the party to educate the Trade Unions in a new manner, distinct from the old one, to guide them, not forgetting meanwhile that they remain and will remain for a long time a necessary "school of Communism," a preparatory school for the training of the proletariat to realise its dictatorship, an indispensable union of the workers for the permanent transference of the management of the country's economic life into their hands as a class (and not to single trades), to be given later into the hands of all the labouring masses.

A certain conservatism of the Trade Unions, in the sense mentioned, is unavoidable under the dictatorship of the proletariat. Not to understand this means completely to fail to understand the fundamental conditions of the transition from capitalism to Socialism. To fear this reactionary tendency, to try to avoid it, to jump over it, is as foolish as it can possibly be; it indicates lack of confidence in the rôle of the proletarian vanguard to train, educate and enlighten, to infuse with new life, the most backward groups and masses of the working class and the peasantry. On the other hand, to postpone the realisation of the proletarian dictatorship until such a time as there is not left a single professionally narrow-minded workman, until all are quite free from craft and Trade Union prejudices, would be a still greater mistake. For a Communist, with a correct understanding of his own ends, the art of politics lies in correctly calculating the conditions and the moment when the proletarian vanguard can take over power successfully. He must decide when, after this assumption of power, that vanguard will be able to obtain adequate support from sufficiently inclusive strata of the working-class and non-proletarian labouring masses, and when it will be able to maintain, consolidate and extend its supremacy, educating, training and attracting ever widening circles of the labouring masses.

In countries more advanced than Russia, a certain reactionary spirit has revealed, and was unquestionably bound to reveal, itself in the Trade Unions much more strongly than in our country. Our Mensheviks had (and in a very few Trade Unions still have) the support of these organisations, just because of their craft narrow-mindedness, professional selfishness, and opportunism. In the west the Mensheviks have acquired a much firmer footing in the Trade Unions. There a much wider stratum of labour aristocracy—those professional, narrow-minded, selfish, brutal, jealous, petit bourgeois elements—has cropped up, imperialistically inclined, and bribed and corrupted by imperialists. That this is so needs no proof. The struggle against Gompers, Jouhaux, Henderson, Merrheim, Legien and Co. in Western Europe is much more difficult than the fight with our Mensheviks, who represent a thoroughly homogeneous social and political type. This struggle must be mercilessly conducted until, as was done in our case, all the incorrigible leaders of opportunism and social-chauvinism have been completely exposed and thrown out of the unions. It is impossible to conquer political power, and the conquest should not even be attempted until this struggle has reached a certain stage. This certain stage must vary in different countries and different circumstances. Only clear-minded, experienced and well-informed political leaders are able to estimate it correctly. In Russia, incidentally, the measure of success in the struggle was gauged by the elections to the Constituent Assembly in November, 1917, a few days after the proletarian revolution of October 25, 1917. In these elections the Mensheviks were totally defeated, having obtained 0.7 million votes (1.4 millions if the vote of Trans-Caucasia be added) as against 9 million votes obtained by the Bolsheviks.*

We carry on the struggle against the labour aristocracy in the name of the working masses, in order to gain them over to our side; and we do battle against the opportunist and social-chauvinist leaders in order to achieve the same object. To forget this most elementary and self-evident truth would be stupid. But the German "Left" Communists commit just this stupidity when, because of the reactionary and counter-revolutionary heads of the Trade Unions, they jump, by some inexplicable mental process, to the conclusion that it is necessary to abandon these organisations altogether! They refuse to work in them! They invent new *invented* working-men's unions! This is an unpardonable blunder, and one by which the Communists render the greatest service to the bourgeoisie. Our Mensheviks, like all opportunist, social-chauvinist Kautskian leaders of Trade Unions, are nothing more nor less than the "agents of the bourgeoisie in the labour movement" (as we always express it), or "labour lieutenants of the capitalist class," according to the excellent and highly expressive summary of the followers of Daniel De Leon in America. Not to work within the reactionary Trade Unions means to leave the insufficiently-developed or backward working masses to the influence of reactionary leaders, agents of the bourgeoisie, labour aristocrats—"bourgeoisified workers." (See Engels' letter to Marx in 1852, concerning British workers.)

It is just this absurd "theory" of non-participation by Communists in reactionary Trade Unions that demonstrates most clearly how light-mindedly these "Left" Communists regard the question of influence over the "masses," how they contradict their own outcries about the "masses." In order to be able to help the "masses" and to win their sympathy, confidence, and support, it is necessary to brave all difficulties, attacks, insults, cavils and persecutions by the leaders (who, being opportunists and social-chauvinists, are, in most cases, directly or indirectly connected with the bourgeoisie and the police), and to work by every possible means wherever the masses are to be found. Great sacrifices must be made, the greatest hindrances must be overcome, in order to carry on agitation and propaganda systematically, stubbornly, insistently, and patiently, in all those institutions, societies, and associations, however reactionary, where proletarians or semi-proletarians gather together. As for Trade Unions and Co-operatives (this applies, at least sometimes, to the

* See my article: " Elections to the Constituent Assembly and the Proletarian Dictatorship," in No. 7–8 of the *Communist International.*

latter), they are just the organisations where the mass is to be found. In Great Britain, according to data given in the Swedish paper, *Folkets Dagblad Politiken,*of March 10, 1919, the Trade Union membership from the end of 1917 to the end of 1918 rose from 5.5 millions to 6.6 millions—*i.e.,* an increase of 19 per cent. Towards the end of 1919, this number reached 7.5 millions. I have not at hand the corresponding data about France and Germany, but the facts testifying to the rapid growth in membership of the Trade Unions in these countries are quite incontestable and are generally known.

These facts speak most clearly, and are confirmed by thousands of other indications, of the growth of class-consciousness, and of the passion for organisation, which exists especially amongst the proletarian masses, in the "rank and file," amongst the backward elements. Millions of workers in England, France and Germany who were not at all organised heretofore have, for the first time, entered the most elementary, most simple and most easily accessible form of organisation—for those still imbued with bourgeois-democratic prejudices—namely, the Trade Unions. And the revolutionary but unwise "Left" Communists stand by, crying "The mass, the mass!" and refuse to work with the Trade Unions; refuse on the pretext of their "conservatism," and contrive new, spick and span "Workers' Unions," guiltless of bourgeois-democratic prejudices, guiltless of craft feeling and narrow professionalism! These Workers' Unions, they claim, will be (will be!) all-embracing, and for participation in them the only (only!) requirement is "the acceptance of the Soviet system and the dictatorship of the proletariat." (See the previous quotation!)

A greater lack of sense and more harm to the revolution than this attitude of the "Left" revolutionaries cannot be imagined. Why, if we in Russia, after two and a-half years of incredible victories over the Russian bourgeoisie and the Entente, had demanded that entrance into the Trade Unions must be conditional upon the "acceptance of the dictatorship," we should have committed a stupid act, impaired our influence over the masses, and helped the Mensheviks. For the whole of the Communist problem is to be able to *convince* the backward, to work in their *midst,* and not to set up a *barrier* between us and them, a barrier of artificial childishly "Left" slogans.

There can be no doubt that Messrs. Gompers, Jouhaux, Henderson, Legien, etc., are very grateful to such "Left" revolutionaries who, like the German "Opposition-in-principle" Party (Heaven preserve us from such "principles") or like revolutionaries in the American "Industrial Workers of the World," preach the necessity of quitting reactionary Trade Unions and of refusing to work in them. Undoubtedly the leaders of opportunism will have recourse to all the tricks of bourgeois diplomacy, will appeal to the help of bourgeois governments, to priests, police, courts, in order to prevent Communists from entering the Trade Unions, by all and every means to put them out, to make their work inside these organisations as unpleasant as possible, to insult, hound and persecute them. It is necessary to be able to withstand all this, to go the whole length of any sacrifice, if need be, to resort to strategy and adroitness, illegal proceedings, reticence and subterfuge, to anything in order to penetrate into the Trade Unions, remain in them, and carry on Communist work inside them, at any cost. Under Czarism until 1905 we had no "legal possibilities," but when Zubatov, the secret service agent, organised Black Hundred workers' meetings and workmen's societies for the purpose of ferreting out revolutionaries and fighting them, we sent members of our party into these meetings and societies. (I personally remember one such comrade, Babushkine, an eminent Petrograd workman, who was shot by the Czar's generals in 1906.) They put us in touch with the masses, acquired much skill in conducting propaganda, and succeeded in wresting the workers from under the influence of Zubatov's agents.* Of course, in Western Europe, which is soaked through and through with inveterate legalist, constitutionalist, bourgeois-democratic prejudices, it is more difficult to carry on such work; but it can and should be carried on, and carried on systematically.

The Executive Committee of the Third International should, in my opinion, directly condemn the policy of non-participation in reactionary Trade Unions; and they should suggest to the next conference of the Communist International the necessity of issuing a general condemnation of such policy, stating in detail the reasons for the irrationality of non-participation and the excessive harm it brings to the cause of the proletarian revolution. They should specify in particular the line of conduct of some Dutch Communists who, whether directly or indirectly, openly or covertly, wholly or partially, supported this erroneous policy. The Third International must break with the tactics of the Second, and not evade or belittle sore points, but face them squarely. The whole truth has been put squarely to the German Independent Social-Democratic Party; the whole truth must likewise be told to the "Left" Communists.

*The Gompers, Hendersons, Jouhaux and Legiens are nothing else than Zubatovs, differing from ours only in their European dress, in the gloss of their civilised, refined, democratically smooth manner of conducting their scoundrelly policy.

7

Should We Participate in Bourgeois Parliaments?

THE German Left Communists, with the greatest contempt—and the greatest lightmindedness—reply to this question in the negative. Their arguments? In the quotation cited above we saw:—"to refuse most decisively any return to the historically and politically worn-out forms of struggle of parliamentarism."

This is said with absurd pretentiousness, and is obviously incorrect. "Return" to parliamentarism! Does that mean that the Soviet Republic already exists in Germany? It does not look as though such were the case. How is it possible, then, to speak of "returning"? Is not this an empty phrase?

Historically, "Parliament has become worn-out"; this is correct as regards propaganda. But everyone knows that it is still very far from being thread-bare when the *practical* question of eliminating Parliament is under consideration. Capitalism could, and very rightly, have been described as "historically worn-out" many decades ago, but this in no way removes the necessity of a very long and very hard struggle against capitalism at the present day. Parliamentarism is "historically worn-out" in a world-historical sense; that is to say, the epoch of bourgeois parliaments has come to an end, the epoch of the proletarian dictatorship has begun. This is incontestably true. But the scale of the world's history is reckoned by decades. Ten or twenty years sooner or later—this from the point of view of the world-historical scale makes no difference, from the point of view of world-history it is a trifle, which cannot be even approximately reckoned. But this is just why it is a crying theoretical mistake to refer, in questions of practical politics, to the world-historical scale.

Parliament is "politically worn-out?" This is quite another matter. If this were true, the position of the "Left" would be strong. Whether it is actually true must be proved by the most searching analysis; the "Left" do not even know how to tackle the problem. In the "theses on Parliamentarism," published in No. 1 of the *Bulletin of the Provisional Amsterdam Bureau of the Communist International*, February, 1920, which obviously expresses Dutch-Left (or Left-Dutch) views, we shall see that the analysis, too, is very poor.

In the first place, the German "Left", as is known, considered parliamentarism "politically worn-out" as far back as January, 1919, contrary to the opinion of such eminent political leaders as Rosa Luxemburg and Karl Liebknecht. It has now been seen that the "Left" made a mistake. This alone radically destroys the proposition that "parliamentarism is politically worn-out." It is incumbent upon the "Left" to prove that their mistake at that time has now ceased to be a mistake. They do not, and cannot, give even the shadow of a proof of their proposition. The attitude of a political party towards its own mistakes is one of the most important and surest criteria of the seriousness of the party, and of how it fulfils in practice its obligations towards its class and towards the labouring masses. To admit a mistake openly, to disclose its reasons, to analyse the surroundings which created it, to study attentively the means of correcting it—these are the signs of a serious party; this means the performance of its duties; this means educating and training the class, and, subsequently, the masses. By neglecting this, by failing to proceed with the utmost care, attention and prudence to investigate their self-evident mistake, the "Left" in Germany (and some in Holland) proved themselves thereby to be not a class *party*, but a circle, not a *party* of the masses, but a group of intellectuals, and a handful of workers who imitate the worst characteristics of the intellectuals.

Secondly, in the same pamphlet of the Frankfurt group of "Left-Wingers," from which we have already cited in detail, we read: "Millions of workmen, still following the policy of the centre" (the Catholic "Centre" Party) "are counter-revolutionary. The village proletarians produce legions of counter-revolutionary troops." (p. 3).

Everything shows that this is said in much too off-hand and exaggerated a manner. But the fact here stated is fundamentally correct, and its acknowledgment by the "Left" goes to prove their mistake with particular clearness. How is it possible to say that "parliamentarism is politically worn-out" when "millions" and "legions" of proletarians not only stand up for parliamentarism generally, but are directly counter-revolutionary? It is clear, then, that parliamentarism in Germany is *not* worn-out politically as yet. It is evident that the "Left" in Germany have mistaken their desire, their ideo-political attitude, for objective reality. This is the most dangerous error which can be made by revolutionaries. In Russia, where the fierce and savage yoke of Tsarism, extending over a long period, had created an extraordinarily great variety of revolutionaries of every creed, remarkable for their wonderful devotion, enthusiasm, strength of mind, and heroism, we watched this mistake particularly closely; and it is because we studied it with particular attention that this mistake is especially familiar to us, and especially apparent to our eyes when revolutionaries in other countries fall into it. For the Communists in Germany parliamentarism *is*, of course, "politically out-worn"; but—and this is the whole point—we must not deem that that which is outworn for us is necessarily outworn for the class, the masses. Here, again, we see that the "Left" do not know how to argue, do not know how to behave as a class, as a party of the masses. True, it is our duty not to sink to the level of the masses, to the level of the backward strata of the class. This is incontestable. It is our duty to tell them the bitter truth. It is our duty to call their bourgeois-democratic and parliamentary prejudices by their right name. But, at the same time, it is our duty to watch soberly the actual state of consciousness and preparedness of the whole class, and not of the Communist vanguard alone; of the whole labouring mass, and not merely of its foremost men.

If, not "millions" and "legions," but merely a considerable *minority* of industrial workers follow the Catholic priests, and if a considerable minority of village workers follow the landowners and rich peasants (grossbauern), it inevitably means that parliamentarism in Germany is *not* politically outworn as yet; hence participation in parliamentary elections and the struggle on the parliamentary platform is *obligatory* for the party of the revolutionary prole-tariat, just for the purpose of educating the backward masses of its own class, just in order to awaken and enlighten the undeveloped, down-trodden, ignorant masses. Just so long as you are unable to disperse the bourgeois parliament and other reactionary institutions, you are *bound* to work inside them, and for the very reason that there are still workmen within them made fools of by priests or by the remoteness of village life. Otherwise you run the risk of becoming mere babblers.

Thirdly, the "Left" Communists have a great deal to say in praise of us Bolsheviks. One sometimes feels like telling them that it were better to praise us less, and go more thoroughly into the tactics of the Bolsheviks, to get better acquainted with them. We participated in the elections to the Russian bourgeois parliament, the Constituent Assembly, in September-November, 1917. Were our tactics right or not? If not, this should be clearly stated and proved; this is essential for the working out of the right tactics for international Communism. If, on the other hand, we were right, certain inferences should be drawn. Of course, there can be no question of approximating Russian conditions to the conditions of Western Europe. But where the special question of the phrase "parliamentarism has become politically outworn" is concerned, it is necessary by all means to gauge our experience; since, without a proper estimate of concrete experiences, such conceptions too easily resolve themselves into empty phrases. Had not we Russian Bolsheviks, in September–November, 1917, more right than any Western Communist to consider that parliamentarism in Russia had become politically outworn? Undoubtedly we had, for the point is not whether bourgeois parliamentarism has existed for a long or a short period, but to what extent the labouring masses are prepared, spiritually, politically and practically to accept the Soviet régime and to disperse (or allow to be dispersed) the bourgeois democratic parliament. That in Russia, in September–November, 1917, the working classes of the towns, the soldiers and the peasants, were, owing to a series of special circumstances, exceptionally well prepared for the accept- ance of the Soviet régime and the dispersal of the democratic bourgeois parliament, is a quite incontestable and fully-established historical fact. However, the Bolsheviks did not boycott the Constituent Assembly, but took part in the elections before, as well as after, the conquest of political power by the proletariat. That these elections gave very valuable (and for the proletariat highly beneficial) political results—this I hope to have proved in the above-mentioned article, which deals in detail with the data concerning the elections to the Constituent Assembly in Russia.

The inference which follows from this is quite clear; it has been proved that participation in bourgeois-democratic parliaments a few weeks before the victory of the Soviet Republic, and even after that victory, not only has not harmed the revolutionary proletariat, but has actually made it easier to prove to the backward masses why such parliaments should be dispersed, has made it easier to disperse them, and has facilitated the process whereby bourgeois parliaments are actually *made* "politically outworn." To pretend to belong to the Communist International, which must work out its tactics internationally (not on narrow national lines), and not to reckon with this experience, is to commit a great blunder, and, while acknowledging inter- nationalism in words, to draw back from it in deeds.

Let us have a look at the arguments of the "Dutch Left" in favour of non- participation in parliaments. Here is the most important of their theses, No. 4:—

> When the capitalist system of production is broken down and society
> is in a state of revolution, parliamentary activity gradually loses its

significance as compared with the action of the masses themselves.
When then under such conditions Parliament becomes the centre and
organ of counter-revolution, while on the other hand the working-
class creates the tools of its power in the shape of Soviets, it may even
become necessary to decline all and any participation in parliamentary
activity.

The first sentence is obviously wrong, since the action of the masses—a
big strike for instance—is more important always than parliamentary
activity, and not merely during a revolution or in a revolutionary situation.
This obviously meaningless argument, historically and politically incorrect,
only shows, with particular clearness, that the authors absolutely ignore
both the general European experience (the French experience before the
revolutions of 1848 and 1870; the German from 1878 to 1890, etc.), and the
Russian, cited above, with regard to the importance of unifying legal and
illegal forms of the struggle. This question has immense significance generally as well as specially. In all civilised and advanced countries, the time is
coming speedily—it may, in fact, be said already to have come—when such
unification becomes more and more—and, to an extent, has already become—
obligatory for the party of the revolutionary proletariat. It is necessitated by
the development and approach of the civil war between the proletariat and
the bourgeoisie, by the furious persecution of Communists by republican
and all bourgeois governments generally, breaking the law in innumerable
ways (the American example alone is invaluable). This most important
question has not been at all understood by these Dutch "Left Communists"
or by the "Left" generally.

The second phrase of the thesis is, in the first place, historically untrue.
We Bolsheviks took part in the most counter-revolutionary Parliaments.
Experience showed that such participation was not only useful, but necessary to the party of the revolutionary proletariat, directly after the first
bourgeois revolution in Russia (in 1905), to prepare the way for the second
bourgeois revolution (February, 1917), and then for the Socialist revolution
(November, 1917). In the second place, this phrase is strikingly illogical. If
Parliament becomes an organ and a "centre" (by the way it never has been in
reality, and never can be, a "centre") of counter-revolution, and the workmen
create the tools of their power in the form of Soviets, it follows that the
workers must prepare themselves—ideologically, politically, technically—
for the struggle of the Soviets against parliament, for the dispersion of

parliament by the Soviets. But it does not at all follow that such a dispersion is made more difficult, or is not facilitated, by the presence of a Soviet opposition within the counter-revolutionary parliament. In the course of our victorious fight against Denikin and Koltchak, it never occurred to us that the existence in their rear of a Soviet, proletarian opposition, was immaterial to our victories. We know perfectly well that the dispersion of the Constituent Assembly on January 5, 1918, was not made more difficult, but was facilitated by the fact that, within the dispersed counter-revolutionary Constituent Assembly, there was a consistent Bolshevik, as well as an inconsistent Left-Social Revolutionary, Soviet opposition. The authors of the theses got into a muddle; they forgot the experience of many, if not all, revolutions, which proved how particularly useful during a revolution is the co-ordination of mass action outside a reactionary parliament with an opposition inside the parliament which sympathises with—or better still directly supports—revolution.

These Dutchmen (and the "Left" in general) altogether argue here as doctrinaires of revolution, who never took part in a real one, or never deeply reflected on the history of the revolution, or naively mistake the subjective "denial" of a certain reactionary institution for its destruction in reality by the united forces of a whole series of objective factors. The surest way of discrediting a new political (and not only political) idea, and to cause it harm, is, under pretext of defending it, to reduce it to an absurdity. For every truth, as Dietzgen senior said, if it be "carried to excess," if it be exaggerated, if it be carried beyond the limits of actual application, can be reduced to an absurdity; and, under the conditions mentioned, is even bound to fall into an absurdity. In their very zeal to help, the Dutch and German "Left" did unwitting harm to the new idea of the superiority of Soviet power over bourgeois-democratic parliaments. Of course, anyone who should say, in the old sweeping way, that refusal to participate in bourgeois parliaments can under no circumstances be permissible, would be wrong. I cannot attempt here to formulate the conditions under which a boycott is useful, for the scope of my article is more limited; here I only want to estimate all the possibilities of Russian experience in connection with certain burning questions of the day, questions of international Communist tactics. Russian experience has given us one successful and correct application of the boycott (1905), and one incorrect application of it, by the Bolsheviks. In the first case we see that we succeeded in preventing the convocation of a reactionary parliament by a reactionary government, under conditions in which revolutionary mass action (strikes in particular) outside parliament was growing with exceptional rapidity. At that time not a single element of the proletariat or the peasantry gave any support to the reactionary government; the proletariat secured for itself influence over the backward masses by means of strike and agrarian movements. It is quite evident that this experience is not applicable to present-day European conditions. It is also quite evident, on the strength of the foregoing arguments, that even a conditional defence of the refusal to participate in parliament, on the part of the Dutch and the "Left," is thoroughly wrong and harmful to the cause of the revolutionary proletariat.

In Western Europe and America, parliament has become an object of special aversion to the advanced revolutionaries of the working class. This is self evident, and is quite comprehensible, for it is difficult to imagine anything more abominable, base, and treacherous than the behaviour of the overwhelming majority of Socialist and Social-Democratic deputies in Parliament, during and after the period of the war. But it would be, not only unreasonable, but obviously criminal to yield to such a frame of mind when solving the question of how to struggle against this generally admitted evil. In many countries of Western Europe the revolutionary mood is, we might say, a "novelty," a "rarity," which has been too long expected, vainly and impatiently it may be; and it may be because of this that people more easily yield to their frame of mind. Of course, without a revolutionary disposition on the part of the masses, and without conditions tending to enhance this disposition, revolutionary tactics will never materialise in action. But we in Russia have convinced ourselves, by long, painful, and bloody experience, of the truth that it is impossible to build up revolutionary tactics solely on revolutionary dispositions and moods.

Tactics should be constructed on a sober and strictly objective consideration of the forces of a given country (and of the countries surrounding it, and of all countries, on a world scale), as well as on an evaluation of the experience of other revolutionary movements. To manifest one's revolutionism solely by dint of swearing at parliamentary opportunism, by rejecting participation in parliaments, is very easy; but, just because it is too easy, it is not the solution of a difficult, a most difficult, problem. In most European states, the creation of a really revolutionary parliamentary group is much more difficult than it was in Russia. Of course. But this is only one aspect of the general truth that it was easy for Russia, in the concrete, historically quite unique, situation of 1917, to begin a social revolution; whereas to continue it and complete it will be more difficult for Russia than for other European countries.

Already at the beginning of 1918 I had occasion to point out this circumstance, and since then an experience of two years entirely corroborates this point of view. Certain specific conditions existed in Russia which do not at present exist in Western Europe, and a repetition of such conditions in another country is not very probable. These specific conditions were (1) the possibility of connecting the Soviet Revolution with the conclusion, thanks to it, of the imperialist war which had exhausted the workers and peasants to an incredible extent; (2) the possibility of making use, for a certain time, of the deadly struggle of two world-powerful groups of imperialist plunderers, who were unable to unite against their Soviet enemy; (3) the possibility of withstanding a comparatively lengthy civil war, partly because of the gigantic dimensions of the country and the bad means of communication; (4) the existence of such a profound bourgeois-revolutionary movement amongst the peasantry that the proletarian party included in its programme the revolutionary demands of the peasant party (the Socialist Revolutionaries, a party sharply hostile to Bolshevism), and at once realised these demands through the proletarian conquest of political power.

The absence of these specific conditions—not to mention various minor ones—accounts for the greater difficulty which Western Europe must experience in beginning the social revolution. To attempt to "circumvent" this difficulty, by "jumping over" the hard task of utilising reactionary parliaments for revolutionary purposes, is absolute childishness. You wish to create a new society? And yet you fear the difficulties entailed in forming, in a reactionary Parliament, a sound group composed of convinced, devoted, heroic Communists! Is not this childishness? Karl Liebknecht in Germany and Z. Höglund in Sweden succeeded, even without the support of the masses from below, in giving examples of a truly revolutionary utilisation of reactionary parliaments. Why, then, should a rapidly-growing revolutionary mass party, under conditions of post-war disappointment and exasperation of the masses, be unable to hammer-out for itself a Communist faction in the worst of parliaments? It is just because, in Western Europe, the backward masses of the workers and the smaller peasantry are much more strongly imbued with bourgeois-democratic and parliamentary prejudices than they are in Russia, that it is only in the midst of such institutions as bourgeois parliaments that Communists can and should carry on their long and stubborn struggle to expose, disperse, and overcome these prejudices, stopping at nothing.

The German "Left" complain of bad "leaders" in their party and give way to despair, going to the length of a laughable "repudiation" of the said "leaders." But when conditions are such that it is often necessary to hide the "leaders" underground, the preparation of good, reliable, experienced and authoritative "leaders" is an especially hard task, and these difficulties cannot be successfully overcome without co-ordinating legal with illegal work, without testing the "leaders" *in the parliamentary arena, among others.* The most merciless, cutting, uncompromising criticism must be directed, not against parliamentarism or parliamentary action, but against those leaders who are unable—and still more against those who do not wish—to utilise parliamentary elections and the parliamentary platform as revolutionaries and Communists should. Only such criticism—added, of course, to the expulsion of worthless leaders and their replacement by capable ones—will constitute useful and fruitful revolutionary work. Thus will both the leaders themselves be trained to become worthy of the working-class and the toiling masses, and the masses learn correctly to understand the political situation, and to understand the often very complicated and intricate problems that originate from such situations.*

---

* I have had very little opportunity to acquaint myself with " Left " Communism in Italy. Unquestionably, Comrade Bordiga and his group of " Communist-Boycottists " (Communista abstentionista) are wrong in defending non-participation in Parliament. But it seems to me—from what I can gather from two issues of his paper, *Il Soviet* (Nos. 3 and 4, January 18 and February 1, 1920), from four issues of Comrade Serrati's excellent periodical *Communismo* (Nos. 1–4, October–November, 1919) and from scattered numbers of Italian bourgeois papers with which I have had the opportunity to acquaint myself—that they are right on one point. Comrade Bordiga and his group are right in their attacks on Turati and his co-thinkers, who remain in a party which has recognised Soviet power and proletarian dictatorship, and who at the same time continue their former detrimental and opportunistic policy as members of parliament. Of course, in suffering this, Serrati and the whole Italian Socialist Party make a mistake which threatens to cause great harm and peril, a peril as great as that in Hungary, where the Hungarian Turatis sabotaged from within both the Party and the Soviet Government. Such a mistaken, inconsistent, or characterless attitude towards the opportunist parliamentarians, on the one hand, creates " Left " Communism, and, on the other, justifies its existence up to a certain point. Comrade Serrati is obviously in the wrong when he accuses Deputy Turati of " inconsistency " (*Communismo*, No. 3); in point of fact, it is the Italian Socialist Party which is inconsistent, in putting up with such opportunist parliamentarians as Turati and Co.

8

No Compromise Whatever?

WE have seen, in the quotation from the Frankfurt pamphlet, with what determination the "Left" put forward this slogan. It is sad to see how men who doubtless consider themselves Marxists, and who desire to be Marxists, have forgotten the fundamental truths of Marxism. This is what was written in 1874 against the Manifesto of thirty-three Communard Blanquists* by Engels, who, like Marx was one of those rarest of authors who in every sentence of every great work show a wonderful profundity of content.

"The German Communists are Communists because, through all intermediary stages and compromises, created not by them, but by the course of historical development, they clearly see and perpetually follow the one final end, the abolition of classes and the creation of a social system in which there will no longer be any place for private property in land or in the means of production. The thirty-three Blanquists are Communists because they imagine that, since *they* want to leap over intermediary stations and compromises, the cause is as good as won, and if (and of this they are firmly convinced) things "begin moving" one of these days, the power will get into their hands, "then Communism will be introduced" the day after to-morrow. Consequently, if this cannot be done immediately, they are not Communists. What a childish naïveté—to put forward one's own impatience as a theoretical argument!"†

In the same article Engels expresses his profound esteem for Vaillant, and speaks of the "undeniable merit" of the latter (who, like Guesde, was one of the most prominent leaders of international Socialism prior to August, 1914, when both turned traitor to the cause of Socialism). But Engels does not leave an apparent mistake without a detailed analysis. Of course, to very young and inexperienced revolutionists, as well as to petit-bourgeois revolutionists (even though very experienced and of a very respectable age), it seems most dangerous, incomprehensible and incorrect to allow compromises.

---

* " We are Communists," wrote the Communard Blanquists in their manifesto, " because we wish to attain our aim directly, without stopping at intermediary stations, without any compromises, which only postpone the day of victory and prolong the period of slavery."

† Fr. Engels' *Programme of the Communard Blanquists*, from the German S.D. paper *Volkstaat*, 1874, No. 73, in the collection of *Articles of the Years* 1871–1875. (*Russian translation*, Petrograd, 1919, pp. 52 and 53.)

And many sophists, by virtue of their being super- or over-"experienced" politicians, reason the same way as the English leaders of Opportunism, mentioned by Comrade Lansbury:—"If the Bolsheviks permit themselves compromises, why should not we be allowed them?" But proletarians, schooled in manifold strikes (to take only this manifestation of the class war), usually comprehend perfectly this most profound (philosophical, historical, political and psychological) truth, as expounded by Engels. Every proletarian who has gone through strikes has experienced compromises with the hated oppressors and exploiters, when the workers had to get back to work, sometimes without obtaining their demands, sometimes consenting to a partial compliance only. Every proletarian, because of that state of the class struggle and intensification of class antagonisms in which he lives, distinguishes between a compromise extorted from him by objective conditions (such as lack of funds in the treasury, no support from without, starvation, and the last stage of exhaustion)—a compromise which in no way lessens the revolutionary devotion and readiness of the worker to continue the struggle—and, on the other hand, the compromise of traitors, who ascribe to objective reasons their own selfishness (strike breakers also effect a "compromise"), to their cowardice, to their desire to fawn upon capitalists, and to their readiness to yield sometimes to threats, sometimes to persuasion, sometimes to sops and flattery on the part of capitalists. Such treacherous compromises are especially plentiful in the history of the English labour movement, made by leaders of the English trade unions; but in one form or another nearly all workers in every country have witnessed similar instances.

To be sure individual cases of exceptional difficulty and intricacy do occur, when it is possible to determine the real character of such a compromise only with the greatest effort; just as there are cases of murder in which it is anything but easy to decide whether the murder was fully justifiable, and, in fact, necessary (as, for example, legitimate self-defence), or an unpardonable piece of negligence, or, again, a skilfully premeditated treacherous plan. Of course, in politics, involving sometimes very intricate national or international relationships between classes and parties, many cases will arise much more difficult than the question of a lawful compromise during a strike, or the treasonable compromise of a strike-breaker, a traitorous leader, etc. To invent such a formula or general rule as "No Compromises," which would serve in all cases, is an absurdity. One must keep one's head in order not to lose oneself in each separate case. Therein, by the way, lies the importance of a party organisation and of party leaders worthy of the name, that, in long, stubborn, varied, and variform struggle, all thinking representatives of a given class may work out the necessary knowledge, the necessary experience, and, apart from all knowledge and experience, the necessary political instincts for the quick and correct solution of intricate political problems.*

Naïve and quite inexperienced persons imagine that it is sufficient to recognise the permissibility of compromise in general, and all differences between opportunism on the one hand (with which we do and must wage uncompromising war) and revolutionary Marxism or Communism on the other will be obliterated. But for those people who do not yet know that all distinctions in nature and in society are unstable (and, to a certain extent, arbitrary), nothing will do but a long process of training, education, enlightenment, political and everyday experience. In practical questions of the policy appropriate to each separate or specific historic moment it is important to be able to distinguish those in which are manifested the main species of inadmissible treacherous compromises, which embody opportunism detrimental to the revolutionary class, and to direct all possible efforts towards elucidating and fighting them. During the imperialist war of 1914-1918, between two groups of equally ruffianly and rapacious countries, such a main fundamental species of opportunism was social-chauvinism, that is, upholding "defence of the Fatherland," which, in such a war, was really equivalent to a defence of the plundering interests of one's own bourgeoisie. Since the war, the defence of the robber "League of Nations"; the defence of direct or indirect alliance with the bourgeoisie of one's country against the revolutionary proletariat and the "Soviet" movement; the defence of bourgeois democracy and bourgeois parliamentarism against "Soviet power"; such are the chief manifestations of those inadmissible and treacherous compromises which, taken all in all, have given rise to an opportunism fatal to the revolutionary proletariat and its cause. "With all determination to reject all compromise with other parties ... all policy of temporising and manœuvring" write the German "Left" in the Frankfurt pamphlet.

It is to be wondered at that, holding such views, the Left do not decisively condemn Bolshevism! Surely it is not possible that the German Left

* So long as classes exist, so long as non-class society has not fully entrenched and consolidated itself, has not developed itself on its own foundations, there inevitably will be in every class, and even in the most enlightened countries, class representatives who neither think nor are capable of thinking. Capitalism would not be the oppressor of the masses that it is, were this not so

were unaware that the whole history of Bolshevism, both before and after the October Revolution, is full of instances of manœuvring, temporising and compromising with others, the bourgeois parties included!

To carry on a war for the overthrow of the international bourgeoisie, a war a hundred times more difficult, prolonged and complicated than the most stubborn of ordinary wars between countries, and to refuse beforehand to manœuvre, to utilise the conflict (even though temporary) of interests between one's enemies; to refuse co-operation and compromise with possible (even though transient, unstable, vacillating, and conditional) allies—is not this an infinitely laughable thing? Is it not as though, in the difficult ascent of an unexplored and heretofore inaccessible mountain, we were to renounce beforehand the idea that we might have to go sometimes in zig-zags, sometimes retracing our steps, sometimes giving up the course once selected and trying various others? And people who are so ignorant and in-experienced (it is all right if this is due to their youth—the Lord Himself has ordained that during a certain time the young should talk such nonsense) are supported in this uncompromising attitude—directly or indirectly, openly or covertly, wholly or partially—by certain Dutch Communists!

After the first Socialist revolution of the proletariat, upon the overthrow of the bourgeoisie in a country, the proletariat remains for a time weaker than the bourgeoisie, simply by virtue of the latter's far-reaching international connections, and also on account of the ceaseless and spontaneous re-birth of capitalism and the bourgeoisie, through the small producers of commodities in the country which has overthrown them. To overcome so potent an enemy is possible only through the greatest effort and by dint of the obligatory, thorough, careful, attentive and skilful utilisation of every breach, however small, between the enemies; of every clash of interests between the bour-geoisie of all countries, between various groups and species of bourgeoisie within individual countries; of every possibility, however small, of gaining an ally, even though he be temporary, shaky, unstable, unreliable and con-ditional. Who has not grasped this has failed to grasp one iota of Marxism and of scientific modern Socialism in general. Whoever has failed to prove in practice, during a considerable period of time and in sufficiently varied political situations, his ability to apply this truth, has not yet learned to aid the revo-lutionary class in its struggle for the liberation of all toiling humanity from its exploiters. All this applies equally to the period before and after the con-quest of political power by the proletariat.

Our theory is not a dogma but a manual of action, said Marx and Engels; and the greatest mistake, the greatest crime of "patented" Marxists like Karl Kautsky, Otto Bauer, etc., is that they have not understood this, that they were unable to apply it in the most important moments of the proletarian revolution. "Political activity is not the pavement of the Nevsky Prospect," (the clean, broad, level pavement of the perfectly straight main street in Petrograd) N. G. Chernishevsky, the great Russian Socialist in the pre-Marxian period, used to say. The Russian revolutionaries, from the time of Chernishevsky, have paid with innumerable victims for ignoring or forgetting this truth. It is necessary by every means to prevent Left Communists and West European and American revolutionaries who are devoted to the working-class from paying as dearly for the assimilation of this truth as did the backward Russians.

Before the downfall of Czarism, the Russian revolutionary Social Democrats made use repeatedly of the service of the bourgeois Liberals—*i.e.*, concluded numerous practical compromises with them. In 1901–2, before the rise of Bolshevism, the old editorial staff of *Iskra* (comprising Plekhanov, Axelrod, Zasulitch, Martov, Potressov, and myself) concluded a formal, although short-lived, political alliance with Struve, the political leader of bourgeois Liberalism, and succeeded at the same time in waging a most merciless ideological and political war against bourgeois Liberalism and against the slightest manifestation of its influence within the working-class movement. The Bolsheviks always continued the same policy. From 1905 they systematically advocated a union of the working class and peasantry against the Liberal bourgeoisie and Czarism. At the same time they never refused to support the bourgeoisie against Czarism (for instance, during the second stage of the election, or in recounts), and never ceased the most irreconcilable ideological and political fight against the bourgeois revolutionary peasant party, the "Socialist Revolutionaries," exposing them as petty bourgeois democrats, falsely masquerading as Socialists.

In 1907 the Bolsheviks, for a short time, formed a formal political bloc in the Duma elections with the "Socialist Revolutionaries." Between 1903 and 1912 we were for several years formally united with the Mensheviks in one Social-Democratic party, never ceasing our ideological and political fight with them, as opportunists and transmitters of bourgeois influence to the proletariat. During the war we accepted some compromise with the "Kautskians," who were partly Left Mensheviks (Martov) and partly "Socialist

Revolutionaries" (Chernov and Natanson), sitting together with them in Zimmerwald and Kienthal, and issuing manifestoes in common; but we never ceased and never slackened our ideologico-political fight with the "Kautskians," Martov and Chernov. (Natanson died in 1919, quite near to us, being a "Revolutionary Communist"—Narodnik—and almost agreeing with us.) At the very moment of the October Revolution we effected an informal (a very important and highly successful) political bloc with the petit bourgeois peasantry, having accepted *fully*, without a single change, the "Socialist Revolutionary" agrarian programme—that is, we effected an undeniable compromise, in order to prove to the peasants that we do not want to dominate them, but to come to an understanding with them. At the same time we proposed, and soon realised, a formal political bloc with the "Left Socialist Revolutionaries," involving working together in the same Government. They broke up this bloc after the conclusion of the Brest Peace, and then went as far as an armed insurrection against us in July, 1918. Subsequently they began an armed struggle against us.

It is therefore comprehensible why all the attacks made by the German "Left" upon the Central Committee of the Communist Party of Germany (because the latter entertained the idea of a bloc with the Independent Social Democratic Party of Germany," the Kautskians) seem to us not at all serious, and prove to us the palpable error of the "Left." We in Russia also had Right Mensheviks (who participated in the Kerensky Government and who correspond to the German Scheidemanns) and Left Mensheviks (Martóv) who were in opposition to the Right Wing, and who correspond to the German Kautskians. We clearly observed, in 1917, how the working masses were gradually abandoning the Mensheviks to come over to the Bolsheviks. At the first All-Russian Congress of Soviets, in June, 1917, we had only 13 %; the majority of votes were for the Socialist Revolutionaries and the Mensheviks. At the Second Congress of Soviets (October 25, 1917—old style) we had 51 %. Why, in Germany, did a wholly similar movement of the workers from Right to Left first strengthen, not the Communists, but the intermediate party of the "Independents"?—although this party never had any independent political idea of its own, no independent policy of its own, but only wavered between the Scheidemanns and the Communists.

Obviously, one of the causes was the *erroneous* tactics of the German Communists, who must fearlessly and honestly admit this mistake and learn to correct it. The mistake consisted in rejecting participation in the reactionary bourgeois parliament and in the reactionary Trade Unions; it consisted in the numerous manifestations of that "Left" infantile disorder which has now appeared on the surface. And the quicker it does so, the better; the more beneficial to the organism will be the cure.

The German "Independent Social-Democratic Party" is obviously not homogeneous. The old opportunist leaders (Kautsky, Hilferding, and, to a considerable extent it seems, Crispien, Ledebour and others), have proven their inability to understand Soviet power and dictatorship of the prole-tariat, their inability to lead the latter in its revolutionary struggle. Side by side with them, there has arisen in this party a Left proletarian wing which is growing with admirable rapidity. Hundreds of thousands of members of this party (and it has, it seems, up to three-quarters of a million members) are proletarians who have left Scheidemann and are marching rapidly to-wards Communism. This proletarian wing has already proposed (at the Liepzig, 1919, Conference of the Independents) an immediate and un-conditional affiliation with the Third International. To fear a "compromise" with this wing of the party is really laughable. On the contrary it is incumbent upon Communists to seek and to *find* an appropriate form of compromise with them; such a compromise as, on the one hand, would facilitate and accelerate the necessary complete fusion with this wing and, on the other, would in no way tie the hands of the Communists in their ideo-political struggle against the opportunist Right wing of the Independents. Probably it will not be easy to work out the appropriate form of compromise, but only a charlatan could promise to the German workmen and Communists an *easy* way to victory.

Capitalism would not be capitalism if the proletariat "pure and simple" were not surrounded by a great many exceedingly variegated and transitory types between the proletarian to the semi-proletarian (who earns a liveli-hood halfway by selling his labour-power); from the semi-proletarian to the small peasant (and small craftsman, handicraft worker, and small master in general); from the small to the middle peasant and so on; and if, within the proletariat itself, there were no divisions into more and less advanced sections—friendly, professional and sometimes religious societies, etc. And this gives rise to the absolute, imperative necessity for the conscious part of the proletarian vanguard, the Communist Party, to resort to manœuvres, temporisings, and compromises with the various groups of proletarians, with the various parties, with the workmen and petty masters.

The whole point lies in being able to apply these tactics to raise and not to lower the general level of proletarian class-consciousness and revolutionary ability to fight and conquer. It is noteworthy, by the way, that the victory of the Bolsheviks over the Mensheviks demanded, not only before the October revolution of 1917, but also after it, the application of such tactics, of manœuvring, temporising and compromise—such, of course, as would facilitate, accelerate, consolidate the Bolsheviks at the expense of the Mensheviks. The petit bourgeois democrats (including the Mensheviks) invariably vacillate between the bourgeoisie and the proletariat, between bourgeois democracy and the Soviet system, between reformism and revolution, between love for the workers and fear of the proletarian dictatorship, etc. The correct tactics of the Communists should consist in utilising these vacillations, and by no means to ignore them. Utilisation demands concessions to the element that turns towards the proletariat. The time, the direction and the extent of these concessions must be determined by circumstances; the questions to be considered being simply when and how far those elements turn towards the proletariat. At the same time a fight must be waged against the elements which turn towards the bourgeoisie. As a result of the application of correct tactics, Menshevism, disintegrated more and more, is now falling to pieces; the obstinately opportunist leaders are being deserted, and the best workers, the best elements from the petit bourgeois democracy, are being brought into our camp. This is a long process, and the hasty decision: "No compromise, no manœuvring" can only prevent the strengthening of the influence of the revolutionary proletariat, and the increasing of its force.

Finally, one of the obvious mistakes of the "Left" in Germany is their unequivocal refusal to recognise the Versailles Treaty. The more "solidly" and "importantly," the more "determinedly" and dogmatically this viewpoint is maintained (by K. Horner, for instance), the less sensible it appears. It is not sufficient, in the present conditions of the international proletarian revolution, to renounce the crying absurdities of "National Bolshevism" (Lauffenberg and others), which has talked itself into a bloc with the German bourgeoisie for war against the Entente. One must understand those tactics to be fundamentally wrong which do not admit that it is necessary for a Soviet Germany (if a German Soviet Republic were shortly to be established) to recognise the Versailles Peace, and to submit to it for a certain time. From this it does not follow that the German "Independents" were right when they demanded the signing of the Versailles Treaty. At that time Scheidemann was in the government; the Soviet Government of Hungary had not yet been overthrown, and there was yet a possibility of a Soviet revolution in Vienna in support of Soviet Hungary. Then the Independents temporised and manœuvred very clumsily, for they more or less took upon themselves the responsibility for the Scheidemann traitors, slipped away, more or less, from the viewpoint of a merciless (and calmly deliberate) class war with the Scheidemanns, and adopted a non-class, or "super-class," viewpoint.

But at present the position is obviously such that the German Communists should not bind themselves hand and foot and take upon themselves the irrevocable obligation of repudiating the Versailles Treaty in the case of the victory of Communism. That would be foolish. One must admit that the Scheidemanns and Kautskians have perpetrated a great many treacheries, obstructing, and in part ruining, the work of union with Soviet Russia and with Soviet Hungary. We Communists will use all means to facilitate and prepare such a union; at the same time, we are not at all bound to repudiate the Versailles Treaty—or, what is more, to repudiate it immediately. The possibility of successfully repudiating the Treaty depends, not only upon the German, but also upon the international success of the Soviet movement. This movement was hampered by the Scheidemanns and Kautskians; we shall help it. Therein lies the main point; that is where the fundamental difference lies. And if our class enemies the exploiters, their lackeys the Scheidemanns and Kautskians, have missed a great many opportunities for strengthening both the German and the international Soviet revolution, the blame falls upon them. The Soviet revolution in Germany will strengthen the international Soviet movement. This is the strongest bulwark—and the only reliable, unconquerable, omnipotent bulwark—against the Versailles Peace, against international imperialism in general. To put the overthrow of the Versailles Peace absolutely and irrevocably in the first place, before the question of the liberation of other countries from the yoke of imperialism, is a species of petit-bourgeois nationalism (worthy of Kautsky, Hilferding, Otto Bauer and Co.) and is not revolutionary internationalism. The overthrow of the bourgeoisie in any of the large European countries, including Germany, is such an accession to the international revolution that for its sake one can, and must if necessary, suffer a longer duration of the Versailles Peace. If Russia by herself, with benefit to the revolution, could endure the Brest Peace for several months, it is not impossible for Soviet Germany, in alliance with Soviet Russia, to suffer, with benefit to the revolution, a still longer duration of the Versailles Treaty.

The imperialists of France, England, etc., are provoking the German Communists, and laying a trap for them. "Say that you will not sign the Peace of Versailles," they say. And the Left Communists, like children, fall into the trap laid for them, instead of manœuvring skilfully against the treacherous and, *for the moment*, stronger enemy; instead of telling him "To-day we shall adhere to the Versailles Treaty." To bind one's hands beforehand, openly to tell the enemy, who is now better armed than we are, whether or not we shall fight him, is stupidity and not revolutionism. To accept battle when this is obviously profitable to the enemy, and not to oneself, is a crime; and those politicians of the revolutionary class who are unable to "manœuvre, temporise, compromise," in order to evade an obviously unprofitable battle, are good for nothing.

9

"Left" Communism in Great Britain.

IN Britain there is as yet no Communist Party,* but there is a young,
extensive, potent Communist movement, rapidly growing among the
workers, which entitles one to entertain the brightest hope. There are,
moreover, several political parties and organisations (the British Socialist
Party, the Socialist Labour Party, the South Wales Socialist Society, and the
Workers' Socialist Federation) which are desirous of forming a Communist
Party and which are carrying on negotiations among themselves to that
effect. In the *Workers' Dreadnought* (Vol. vi, No. 48, February 21, 1920), the
weekly organ of the last of the above-named organisations, edited by Comrade
Sylvia Pankhurst, she publishes an article "Towards the Communist Party."
The article describes the course of negotiations between the four above-
mentioned organisations regarding the formation of a single Communist
Party on the basis of affiliation to the Third International, acknowledgment
of the Soviet System instead of parliamentarism, and the dictatorship of the
proletariat. It appears that one of the chief obstacles to the immediate creation
of a single Communist Party is the difference of opinion on the question of
participation in Parliament, and on the affiliation of the new Communist
Party to the old professionalist Labour Party, composed of Trade Unions,
opportunist, and social-chauvinist. The Workers' Socialist Federation, as
well as the Socialist Labour Party,† are against participation in Parliament and
Parliamentary elections; they are also against affiliation to the Labour Party,
disagreeing in this respect with all, or a majority of, the members of the
British Socialist Party—"the right wing of the Communist parties in
England," according to the editor's way of looking at it.

Thus the principal division here is the same as in Germany, notwithstanding the enormous differences in the way in which these differences
manifest themselves, and a whole series of other circumstances. In Germany
this form much more nearly approaches the Russian than in England. Let
us have a look at the arguments of the "Left."

On the question of participation in Parliament, Comrade Sylvia Pank-

* Written before the formation of the Communist Party of Great Britain in August,
1920.
† I believe this party (the S.L.P.) is against affiliation with the Labour Party, but not
all of its members oppose participation in Parliament

hurst refers to an article of Comrade W. Gallacher, printed in the same issue, who writes in the name of the Scottish Workers' Committee of Glasgow:

"This Committee (S.W.C.) is definitely anti-Parliamentarian, and has behind it the Left wing of the various political bodies.

"We represent the revolutionary movement in Scotland, striving continually to build up a revolutionary organisation within the different branches of industry, and a Communist Party, based on social committees, throughout the country. For a considerable time we have been sparring with the official parliamentarians. We have not considered it necessary to declare open warfare on them, and they are *afraid* to open an attack on us.

"But this state of affairs cannot continue long. We are winning all along the line. The rank and file of the I.L.P. in Scotland is becoming more and more disgusted with the idea of Parliament, and the Soviets or Workers' Councils are being supported by almost every branch.

"This is very serious, of course, for the gentlemen who look to politics for a profession, and they are using any and every means to persuade their members to come back into the Parliamentary fold. Revolutionary comrades *must* not give any support to this gang. Our fight here is going to be a difficult one. One of the worst features of it will be the treachery of those whose personal ambition is a more compelling force than their regard for the revolution.

"Any support given to Parliamentarism is simply helping to put power into the hands of our British Scheidemanns and Noskes. Henderson, Clynes and Co. are hopelessly reactionary. The official I.L.P. is more and more coming under the control of middle-class Liberals, who, since the rout of the Liberal Party, have found their 'spiritual home' in the camp of Messrs. MacDonald, Snowden and Co. The official I.L.P. is bitterly hostile to the Third International, the rank and file is for it. Any support to the Parliamentary opportunists is simply playing into the hands of the former.

"The B.S.P. here simply cuts no ice . . . . .

"What is wanted here is a sound, revolutionary, industrial organisation and a Communist Party working along clear, well-defined, scientific lines. If our comrades can assist us in building these, we will take their help gladly; if they cannot, for God's sake let them keep out altogether, lest they betray the Revolution by lending their support to the reactionaries, who are so eagerly clamouring for Parliamentary ' honours ' (?—the query belongs to the author of the letter), and who are so anxious to prove that they can rule as effectively as the ' Boss' class politicians themselves."

This letter to the editor splendidly expresses, in my opinion, the frame of mind and the viewpoint of young Communists, or of the rank and file of the workers who have just begun to arrive at Communism. This frame of mind is highly welcome and valuable; it is necessary to appreciate and support it, as, without it, the victory of the proletarian revolution in Britain, or in any other country, would be hopeless. People who are able to express such a disposition of the masses, who are able to awaken in them such a mood (which often lies dormant, unconscious, and unawakened) should be cared for attentively and every assistance rendered them. At the same time, they must be told, frankly and openly, that that mood alone is not sufficient to guide the masses in the great revolutionary struggle, and that people devoted to the cause of the revolution may make mistakes which do actual harm to that cause itself. Comrade Gallacher's letter to the editor reveals, without doubt, in embryo *all* the errors which are being made by the German "Left" Communists, and which were committed by the Russian "Left" Bolsheviks in the years 1908 and 1918.

The author of the letter is full of the noblest proletarian hate towards class politicians of the bourgeoisie; and his hate is comprehensible and dear, not only to the proletariat, but to all toilers, to all "little people," to use the German expression. This hatred of the representative of oppressed and exploited masses is, indeed, "the beginning of all wisdom"; it is the basis of every Socialist and Communist movement and of its success. The author, however, evidently does not take into consideration the fact that politics is a science and an art which does not drop from the skies, and which cannot be obtained for nothing; and that the proletariat, if it wishes to overcome the bourgeoisie, must create for itself its own, proletarian, "class politicians," as capable as bourgeois politicians.

The author of the letter has understood excellently that not Parliament but Workers' Councils will be the way by which the proletariat will achieve its end; of course, those who have not yet understood this are the most vicious reactionaries, even though they be the most learned men, the most erudite Marxists, the most honest citizens and fathers of families. The author of the letter does not, however, even think of putting the question as to whether or not it is possible for the Soviets to vanquish Parliament without introducing "Soviet" workers into the latter, without disintegrating Parliament from within, without preparing inside Parliament the success of Soviets in the impending struggle for the dispersion of Parliaments. At the same time, however, the author of the letter expresses the thoroughly right idea that the Communist Party in England must act upon a scientific basis. Science demands, in the first place, an evaluation of the experience of other countries, especially if those others are undergoing or have recently undergone a very similar experience; in the second place, it demands an evaluation of all forces, groups, parties, classes, masses, acting within the given country, and the determination of one's policy not merely according to the strength of the desires and views of one group or party, according to its degree of class consciousness and readiness for the struggle.

That the Hendersons, Clynes, MacDonalds and Snowdens are hopelessly reactionary is true. It is also true that they want to take the power into their own hands (preferring, however, a coalition with the bourgeoisie), that they want to govern according to the same old rules of the bourgeoisie, and that they will inevitably behave, when in power, like the Scheidemanns and the Noskes. All this is true, but it does not necessarily follow that to support them means treason to the revolution; on the contrary, in the interests of the revolution, the revolutionaries of the working class must render to these gentlemen a certain parliamentary support.

To make this thought clearer, I shall take two contemporary English political documents, (1) the speech of Lloyd George, on March 18, 1920, as published in the *Manchester Guardian* of the following day, and (2) the arguments of the "Left" Communist, Comrade Sylvia Pankhurst, in her above-mentioned article.

Lloyd George in his speech argued against Asquith (who was specially invited to the meeting, but refused to appear) and those Liberals who desire, not a coalition with the Conservatives, but a closer connection with the Labour Party. (In the letter of Comrade Gallacher we also find mention of the fact that Liberals are going over to the Independent Labour Party.) Lloyd George sought to prove that a coalition of the Liberals with the Conservatives, and a close one at that, was necessary, otherwise victory would be on the side of the Labour Party, which Lloyd George prefers to call "Socialist," and which strives towards collective ownership of the means of production. "In France it was known as Communism," the leader of the English bourgeoisie explained to his hearers (members of the Liberal Party who probably up to that time had been unaware of it), "in Germany it was known as Socialism, and in Russia it is known as Bolshevism." For the Liberals, explained Lloyd George, this is unacceptable on principle, as the Liberals on principle are for private property. "Civilisation is in jeopardy," declared the orator, and, therefore, the Liberals and Conservatives must unite.

"If you go to the agricultural areas," said Lloyd George, "I agree that you have the old party divisions as strong as ever; they are far removed from the danger. It does not walk in their lanes. But when they see it they will be as strong as some of these industrial constituencies now are. Four-fifths of this country is industrial and commercial; hardly one-fifth is agricultural. It is one of the things I have constantly in my mind when I think of the dangers of the future here. In France the population is agricultural, and you have a solid body of opinion which does not move very rapidly, and which is not easily excited by revolutionary movements. That is not the case here. This country is more top-heavy than any country in the world, and if it begins to rock, the crash here, for that reason, will be greater than in any other land."

The reader sees from this that Mr. Lloyd George is not only a very clever man, but that he has learned much from the Marxists. It would not be committing a sin for us to learn something from Mr. Lloyd George.

It is interesting to note the following question put after Mr. Lloyd George's speech:—Mr. WALLACE: "I should like to ask what the Prime Minister considers the effect might be in the industrial constituencies upon the industrial workers, so many of whom are Liberals at the present time and from whom we get so much support. Would not a possible result be to cause an immediate overwhelming accession of strength to the Labour Party from men who, at the present time, are our cordial supporters"? The PRIME MINISTER: "I take a totally different view. The fact that Liberals are fighting among themselves undoubtedly drives a very considerable number of Liberals in despair to the Labour Party, where you get a considerable body of Liberals, very able men, whose business it is to discredit the Government. The result is undoubtedly to bring a good accession of public sentiment to the Labour Party. It does not go to the Liberals who are outside, it goes to the Labour Party, the by-elections show that."

By way of remark this discussion specially shows how the cleverest of the bourgeoisie have got into a muddle, and cannot help committing irreparable blunders. It is from this that the bourgeoisie will perish. Our people may commit stupidities, it is true, but so long as these stupidities be not vital and be corrected in time, we shall none the less conquer in the end.

Another political document gives the following arguments of the "Left" Communist, Comrade Sylvia Pankhurst:—

Comrade Inkpin (secretary of the British Socialist Party) refers to the Labour Party as "the main body of the working-class movement." Another comrade of the B.S.P., at the conference of the Third International just held, put the B.S.P. position more strongly. He said: "We regard the Labour Party as the organised working class."

We do not take this view of the Labour Party. The Labour Party is very large numerically, though its membership is to a great extent quiescent and apathetic, consisting of men and women who have joined the Trade Unions because their workmates are Trade Unionists and to share the friendly benefits. But we recognise that the great size of the Labour Party is also due to the fact that it is the creation of a school of thought beyond which the majority of the British working class has not yet emerged, though great changes are at work in the minds of the people, which will presently alter this state of affairs. The British Labour Party, like the social-patriotic organisations of other countries, will, in the natural development of society, inevitably come into power. It is for the Communists to build up the forces which will overthrow the social-patriots, and in this country we must not delay or falter in that work.

We must not dissipate our energy in adding to the strength of the Labour Party; its rise to power is inevitable. We must concentrate on making a Communist movement that will vanquish it. The Labour Party will soon be forming a government; the revolutionary opposition must get ready to attack it.

And so, the Liberal bourgeoisie renounce the bi-party system of the exploiters—historically sanctified by centuries of experience, and highly profitable to the exploiters—finding it necessary to join their forces for the fight against the Labour Party. Part of the Liberals, like rats deserting a sinking ship, run over to the Labour Party. The Left Communists find it inevitable that the power will fall into the hands of the Labour Party, and admit that at the present time the latter is backed by a majority of working men. From this they draw the strange conclusion which Comrade Sylvia Pankhurst expresses as follows:—

A Communist Party must not enter into compromises. . . . A Communist Party must keep its doctrine pure, and its independence of reformism inviolate; its mission is to lead the way, without stopping or turning, by the direct road to the Communist revolution.

On the contrary, since the majority of the workers in Britain still support the British Scheidemanns and Kerenskys; since they have not yet experienced a government composed of such men, which experience was necessary in Russia and Germany before there was an exodus of the masses towards Communism, it follows without any doubt that the British Communists must participate in Parliament. They must from *within* Parliament help the workers to see in practice the results of the Henderson and Snowden government; they must help the Hendersons and Snowdens to vanquish Lloyd George and Churchill united. To act otherwise means to hamper the progress of the revolution; because, without an alteration in the views of the majority of the working class, revolution is impossible; and this change can be brought about by the political experience of the masses only, and never through propaganda alone. If an indisputably weak minority of the workers say "Forward, without compromise, without stopping or turning," their slogan is, on the face of it, wrong. They know, or at least they should know, that the majority, in the event of Henderson's and Snowden's victory over Lloyd George and Churchill, will, after a short time, be disappointed in its leaders, and will come over to Communism—or at any rate to neutrality and, in most cases, to benevolent neutrality towards the Communists. It is as though ten thousand soldiers were to throw themselves into battle against fifty thousand of the enemy at a time when a reinforcement of one hundred thousand men is expected but is not immediately available; obviously, it is necessary at such a moment to stop, to turn, even to effect a compromise. This no-compromise slogan is intellectual childishness, and not the serious tactics of the revolutionary class.

The fundamental law of revolution confirmed by all revolutions, and particularly by all three Russian revolutions of the twentieth century, is as follows: It is not sufficient for the revolution that the exploited and oppressed masses understand the impossibility of living in the old way and demand changes; for the revolution it is necessary that the exploiters should not be able to live and rule as of old. Only when the masses *do not want* the old regime, and when the rulers *are unable* to govern as of old, then only can the revolution succeed. This truth may be expressed in other words: revolution is impossible without an all-national crisis, affecting both the exploited and the exploiters. It follows that for the revolution it is essential, first, that a

E

majority of the workers (or at least a majority of the conscious, thinking, politically active workers) should fully understand the necessity for a revolution, and be ready to sacrifice their lives for it; second, that the ruling class be in a state of governmental crisis which attracts even the most backward masses into politics. It is a sign of every real revolution, this rapid tenfold, or even hundredfold, increase in the number of representatives of the toiling and oppressed masses, heretofore apathetic, who are able to carry on a political fight which weakens the government and facilitates its overthrow by the revolutionaries.

In Britain, as is seen specifically from Lloyd George's speech, both conditions for a successful proletarian revolution are obviously developing. And mistakes on the part of the Left Communists are now all the more dangerous just because some revolutionaries show an insufficiently penetrating, insufficiently attentive, conscious and foreseeing attitude, towards each of these conditions. If we are not a revolutionary group, but a party of the revolutionary class, and wish to carry the masses with us (without which we run the risk of remaining mere babblers), we must first help Henderson and Snowden to defeat Lloyd George and Churchill; or, to be more explicit, we must *compel* the former to defeat the latter, for the former are afraid of their victory! Secondly, we must help the majority of the working class to convince themselves, through their own experience, that we are right; that is, they must convince themselves of the utter worthlessness of the Hendersons and Snowdens, of their petit-bourgeois and treacherous natures, of the inevitability of their bankruptcy. Thirdly, we must accelerate the moment when, through the disappointment of the majority of the workers with the Hendersons, it will be possible, with serious chances of success, to overthrow the Henderson government—which will most certainly lose its head if the clever leader of, not the petit, but grand bourgeoisie, Lloyd George himself, loses his wits so completely and more weakens himself—and with himself the whole bourgeois party—yesterday through his "collisions" with Churchill, to-day with his "collisions" with Asquith.

Let me speak more concretely. The British Communists must, in my opinion, unite all their four parties and groups (all of them very weak, some very, very weak into one single Communist Party, on the platform of the principles of the Third International, with *obligatory* participation in Parliament. The Communist Party must offer to the Hendersons and Snowdens a compromise, an electoral understanding:—"Let us go together against the union of Lloyd George and Churchill; let us divide the seats in Parliament according to the number of votes cast by the workers for the Labour Party or the Communists (not in the elections but by a special poll), we to retain the fullest freedom of agitation, propaganda, and political activity." Without the latter condition there can, of course, be no bloc, for this would be treason; the British Communists must and will stand up for and maintain the fullest liberty in exposing the Hendersons and Snowdens, as did the Russian Bolsheviks for fifteen years (1903–1917) in relation to the Russian Hendersons and Snowdens, that is, the Mensheviks.

If the Hendersons and Snowdens accept the bloc on these conditions, then we are the gainers, for it is altogether immaterial how many seats in Parliament we get. On this point we shall make more concessions so long as the Hendersons, and especially their new friends (or should it be their new masters?) the Liberals, who have gone over to the Independent Labour Party —are keenest on this. We are the gainers, for we shall carry our propaganda into the masses at the very moment when Lloyd George himself has thrown the Labour Party a challenge; and we shall help, not only the Labour Party to form its Government the more speedily, but also the masses the sooner to understand our Communist propaganda, which we shall carry on ceaselessly against the Hendersons, overlooking nothing.

If the Hendersons and Snowdens reject a bloc on these conditions, we shall gain still more. For we have at once thus shown to the masses that the Hendersons prefer their own nearness to the capitalists to the unification of all the workers. In this connection it is to be noticed that even in purely Menshevik circles—*i.e.,* the entirely opportunist Independent Labour Party—the rank and file are for Soviets. We have at once gained in the eyes of the masses; they, after the highly accurate exposure of Lloyd George— highly useful for Communists—will sympathise with the unification of all workers against the coalition of Lloyd George and Churchill. We score again in demonstrating that the Hendersons and Snowdens are afraid to defeat Lloyd George, are afraid to take the power alone, and are striving *secretly* to gain the support of Lloyd George, who is *openly* stretching a hand to Churchill against the Labour Party.

It should be noted that in Russia, after the revolution of February 27, 1917 (old style), the propaganda of the Bolsheviks against the Mensheviks and Socialist Revolutionaries (*i.e.,* the Russian Hendersons and Snowdens) gained on account of precisely similar circumstances. We said to the Mensheviks and Social Revolutionaries: "Take the whole power without the bourgeoisie, for you have a majority in the Soviets." (At the First All-Russian Congress of Soviets, in June, 1917, the Bolsheviks had only 13 per cent. of the votes.) But the Russian Hendersons and Snowdens feared to take the power without the bourgeoisie. Consequently, when the latter kept delaying the elections to the Constituent Assembly (knowing full well that the majority of votes would go to the Social Revolutionaries and the Mensheviks, which parties were in the closest political bloc and represented in fact one petit bourgeois democracy), they (the Socialist Revolutionaries and Mensheviks) were powerless to fight energetically against these delays.*

Should the Hendersons and Snowdens refuse to form a bloc with the Communists, the latter would have at once gained in the work of obtaining the sympathies of the masses and of discrediting the Hendersons and Snowdens; and if, on that account, the Communists should lose a few seats in Parliament, it would not matter very much to them. We would put forward our candidates only in very insignificant numbers, and only in absolutely safe districts, *i.e.,* where our candidate would not help to elect a Liberal against a Labourite. We would carry on an election campaign, spreading literature in favour of Communism, and proposing in all districts where we have no candidates to vote for the Labourite against the bourgeois. Comrades Sylvia Pankhurst and Gallacher are mistaken if they think there is treason to Communism in this, or that it signifies the renunciation of the fight against social traitors. On the contrary, the cause of the Communist revolution could undoubtedly only gain by this.

At present it is often difficult for the British Communists even to approach the masses, even to make themselves heard. But if I address the masses as a Communist, and invite them to vote for Henderson against Lloyd George, I most certainly will be listened to. And, being listened to, I shall be able to popularise the idea, not only that Soviets are better than Parliaments, and that the dictatorship of the proletariat is better than the dictatorship of Churchill (disguised under the name of bourgeois "democracy"), but also that I am prepared to support Henderson by my vote in just the same way as a rope supports the man who has hanged himself. And, as the Hendersons draw nearer to the formation of their own government, it will be proved that I am right, it will draw the masses to my side, and will facilitate the political death

---

* The elections to the Constituent Assembly in Russia in November, 1917, on a poll comprising more than thirty-six million electors, gave 25 per cent. of the votes to the Bolsheviks, 13 per cent. to the various parties of landlords and bourgeoisie, and 62 per cent. to petit-bourgeois democracy—*i.e.,* to Socialist Revolutionaries and Mensheviks, together with small kindred groups.

of the Hendersons and Snowdens, as happened in the case of their co-thinkers in Russia and in Germany.

And if the objection be raised: "These are too cunning and intricate tactics; the masses won't understand them; they scatter and disintegrate our forces; they will interfere with concentration on the Soviet revolution, etc.;" I shall reply to the "Left" critics: "Don't attribute your doctrinairism to the masses!" It is a matter of fact that the masses in Russia are not more but less advanced than in England; nevertheless, the masses did understand the Bolsheviks, and the latter were helped, not hindered, by the circumstances that, on the eve of the Soviet Revolution, in September, 1917, lists of their candidates for the bourgeois parliament (Constituent Assembly) were being prepared, and that on the *morrow* of the Soviet Revolution, in November, 1917, they were taking part in elections to the very same Constituent Assembly which, on January 5, 1918, was dispersed by them.

I cannot dwell here on the second point at issue between the British Communists; that is, the question of affiliation or non-affiliation to the Labour Party. I have too little information on this question, which is especially complicated on account of the quite unique composition of the British Labour Party, which is so very unlike the composition of the usual political parties on the Continent.

I have no doubt, however, that, on this question as well, he would be mistaken who would be inclined to draw up the tactics of the revolutionary proletariat on the principle that "the Communist Party must maintain its doctrine pure and its freedom from reformism inviolate; its slogan must be to go forward without stopping or turning aside, to follow the straight road to the Communist revolution." For such principles only repeat the mistakes of the French Communard-Blanquists who, in the year 1874, proclaimed the "repudiation" of all compromises and of all intermediary positions. Secondly, it is beyond question that the problem, here as everywhere, consists in the ability to apply the general and fundamental principles of Communism to the specific relations between classes and parties, to the specific conditions in the objective development towards Communism—conditions which are peculiar to every separate country, and which one must be able to study, understand, and point out.

But of this we shall have to speak not only in connection with British Communism, but in connection with the general conclusions pertaining to the development of Communism in all capitalist countries. These we shall now take up.

10

Some Conclusions.

THE Russian bourgeois revolution of 1905 stands out in one respect as a unique turning-point in the world's history. In one of the most backward capitalist countries, a strike movement developed which was unprecedented for its extent and strength. During the first *month* of 1905, the number of strikers was ten times the average *yearly* number for the previous ten years (1895–1904) and, from January to October, 1905, strikes grew continuously and in tremendous dimensions. Backward Russia, under the influence of a great many quite peculiar historical conditions, was the first to show to the world, not only the wave-like growth of the activity of the oppressed masses during the revolution—a feature common to all great revolutions—but also the importance of the proletariat, infinitely greater than its numerical position in the population. It showed the world the blending of the economic and political strikes, the latter transforming itself into armed insurrection; it showed the birth of a new form of mass action and mass organisation of the classes oppressed by capitalism—*i.e.*, the Soviets.

The February and October revolutions of 1917 brought the Soviets to complete development on a national scale, and subsequently to their victory in the proletarian Socialist revolution. And, less than two years after, the international character of the Soviets revealed itself in the spread of this form of organisation over the world-wide struggle of the working class. It became apparent that the historical mission of the Soviets was to be the grave-digger, the heir and the successor of bourgeois parliamentarism, and bourgeois democracy generally.

Furthermore, the history of the working-class movement now shows that in all countries it must experience (and has already begun to experience) a struggle before it grows and strengthens towards the victory of Communism. The struggle is, first and foremost, with the opportunism and social-chauvinism of the "Menshevik" element in its particular country; secondly, the struggle is, in some sort, with "Left" Communism. The first stage of this struggle has developed itself in all countries, without, it seems, a single exception, as the fight between the Second (now practically killed) and Third Internationals. The second stage of the struggle can be observed in Germany, in England, in Italy and in America (at least a certain part of the Industrial

Workers of the World and the anarcho-syndicalist elements in America defend the errors of "Left" Communism side by side with an almost general, almost unconditional acceptance of the Soviet system). This phase of the struggle can also be observed in France, where the hostile attitude of a part of the former Syndicalists towards the political party and parliamentary action exists side by side with the recognition of the Soviets. This similarity makes the struggle against "Left" Communism not only international but also world-wide in its scope.

But, while it everywhere goes through substantially the same training school for victory over the bourgeoisie, the Labour movement of each country effects this development after its own manner. The big advanced capitalist countries progress along the road much more rapidly than did the Bolsheviks, who were granted by history a period of fifteen years to prepare for victory as an organised political force. The Third International, within the short space of one year, has already scored a decisive victory, has defeated the yellow, social-chauvinist Second International. Only a few months ago the latter was incomparably stronger than the Third; it appeared stable and potent; it enjoyed support from all sides, direct material assistance (Ministerial posts, passports, the Press) as well as the moral support of the bourgeoisie all over the world. To-day it is dying.

The main thing now is that the Communists of each country should, in full consciousness, study both the fundamental problems of the struggle with opportunism and "Left" doctrinairism, and the specific peculiarities which this struggle inevitably assumes in each separate country, according to the idiosyncrasies of its politics, economics, culture, national composition (*e.g.*, Ireland), its colonies, religious divisions, etc. Everywhere is felt an ever-widening and increasing dissatisfaction with the Second International, a dissatisfaction due to its opportunism and its incapacity to create a real leading centre, able to direct the international tactics of the revolutionary proletariat in the struggle for the world Soviet Republic. One must clearly realise that such a leading centre can, under no circumstances, be built after a single model, by a mechanical adjustment and equalisation of the tactical rules of the struggle. The national and State differences, now existing between peoples and countries, will continue to exist for a very long time, even after the realisation of the proletarian dictatorship on a world scale. Unity of international tactics in the Communist Labour movement everywhere demands, not the elimination of variety, not the abolition of the national peculiarities (this at the present moment is a foolish dream), but such an application of the fundamental principles of Communism—Soviet power and the Dictatorship of the Proletariat—as will admit of the right modification of these principles, in their adaptation and application to national and national-State differences. The principal problem of the historical moment in which all advanced (and not only the advanced) countries now find themselves lies here; that specific national peculiarities must be studied, ascertained, and grasped before concrete attempts are made in any country to solve the aspects of the single international problem, to overcome opportunism and Left doctrinairism within the working-class movement, to overthrow the bourgeoisie, and to institute a Soviet Republic and proletarian dictatorship.

The main thing—although far from everything—has already been achieved in winning over the vanguard of the working class, in winning it over to the side of Soviet power against parliamentarism, to the side of proletarian dictatorship against bourgeois democracy. Now all efforts, all attention, must be concentrated on the next step, which seems, and from a certain standpoint really is, less fundamental, but which is, in fact, much nearer to a practical solution of the proletarian revolution. That step is to discover the forms of *approach* or *transition* to the proletarian revolution.

The proletarian vanguard has been won over to our ideas. That is the main thing. Without this, not even the first step to victory can be taken, but victory is still distant. With the vanguard alone, victory is impossible. It would be not only foolish, but criminal, to throw the vanguard into the final struggle so long as the whole class, the general mass, has not taken up a position either of direct support of the vanguard or at least of benevolent neutrality towards it, so long as all probability of its supporting the enemy is not past. And, in order that really the whole class, the general mass, of toilers oppressed by capitalism may come to such a position, propaganda and agitation alone are not sufficient. For this, the masses must have their own political experience. Such is the fundamental law of all great revolutions, now confirmed with striking force and vividness, not only in Russia, but also in Germany. It has been necessary, not only for the backward, often illiterate, masses of Russia, but for the highly cultured, entirely literate masses of Germany as well, to realise, through their own suffering, the impotence and characterlessness, the helplessness and servility before the bourgeoisie, the dastardliness of the government of the knights of the Second International, the inevitability of a choice between the dictatorship of the extreme reactionaries (Kornilov in Russia, Kapp and Co. in Germany), and the complete dictatorship of the proletariat—in order to turn them resolutely towards Communism.

The problem of the day for a class-conscious vanguard in the international labour movement (*i.e.*, for the Communist Parties and those groups with Communist tendencies) is to be able to bring the general mass—still, in the majority of cases, slumbering, apathetic, hidebound and ignorant—to their new position; it is to be able to lead, not only their own party, but also the masses, during the transitional period. Some feel that the first problem— that of gaining the conscious vanguard of the working-class to the side of Soviet power and proletarian dictatorship—is impossible to solve without a complete ideological and political victory over opportunism and social-chauvinism. If this is so, the second problem—that of bringing the *masses* over to their new position, which alone can assure the victory of the vanguard in the revolution—cannot be solved without the liquidation of Left doctrinairism, without completely overcoming and getting rid of its mistakes.

So long as the question was, and still is, one of gaining the vanguard of the proletariat for Communism, just so long and so far will propaganda take the first place; even sectarian circles, with all the imperfections of sectarianism, here give useful and truthful results. But when the question is one of the practical activities of the masses, of the disposition—if it be permissible to use this expression—of armies numbering millions and of the distribution of all the class forces of a given society, for the last and decisive fight, here propaganda alone, the mere repetition of the truths of "pure" Communism, will avail nothing. Here one must count by millions and tens of millions, not by thousands, as, after all, the propagandist does, the member of a small group that never yet led the masses. Here one must ask oneself, not only whether the vanguard of the revolutionary class has been convinced, but also whether the historically active forces of *all* classes of a given society have been properly distributed, so that the final battle may not be premature. One must make sure, first, that all the class forces hostile to us have fallen into complete enough confusion, are sufficiently at loggerheads with each other, have sufficiently weakened themselves in a struggle beyond their capacities, to give us a chance of victory; secondly, one must ensure that all the vacillating, wavering, unstable, intermediate elements—the petit bourgeoisie and the petit-bourgeois democracy, in contradistinction to the bourgeoisie—have sufficiently exposed themselves in the eyes of the people, and have disgraced themselves through their material bankruptcy; thirdly, one must have the feeling of the masses in favour of supporting the most determined, unselfishly resolute, revolutionary action against the bourgeoisie.

Then, indeed, revolution is ripe; then, indeed, if we have correctly gauged all the conditions briefly outlined above, and if we have chosen the moment rightly, our victory is assured.

The differences between the Churchills and Lloyd Georges (these political types exist in all countries, allowing for trifling national variations) and between the Hendersons and Lloyd Georges are quite unimportant and shallow from the viewpoint of pure—*i.e.,* of *abstract* Communism, that is, of Communism which has not yet ripened into practical mass political activity. But from the viewpoint of the practical activity of the masses, these differences are exceedingly important. The Communist who wishes to be not only a class-conscious convinced propagandist, but a practical leader of the masses in the revolution, must carefully estimate these differences, and determine the moment of the complete maturity of the conflicts which inevitably weaken and debilitate all these "friends"; herein lies his whole work, his whole problem. It is necessary to co-ordinate the strictest devotion to the ideas of Communism with the ability to accept all necessary practical compromises, manœuvrings, temporisings, zig-zags, retreats and the like. This co-ordination is essential in order to hasten the rise and fall, the realisation and the withering away, of the political power of the Hendersons (the heroes of the Second International, to mention no names, the representatives of the petit bourgeois democracy who call themselves Socialists); it is essential in order to facilitate their inevitable practical bankruptcy, which enlightens the masses precisely after our ideas, precisely in the direction of Communism. One must precipitate the inevitable quarrel and conflicts between the Hendersons, Lloyd Georges and Churchills (Mensheviks, Socialist Revolutionaries, Cadets and Monarchists; Scheidemanns, bourgeoisie, and Kapps, etc.) and choose correctly the moment of the maximum disintegration between all these "buttresses of sacred private property," in order to defeat them all in one decisive offensive of the proletariat, and conquer political power.

History in general, the history of revolutions in particular, has always been richer, more varied and variform, more vital and "cunning" than is conceived of by the best parties, by the most conscious vanguards of the most advanced classes. This is natural, for the best vanguards express the consciousness, will, passions and fancies of but tens of thousands, whereas the revolution is effected at the moment of the exceptional uplift and exertion of *all* the human faculties—consciousness, will, passion, phantasy—of tens of millions, spurred on by the bitterest class war. From this there follow two very important practical conclusions; first, the revolutionary class, for the realisation of its object, must be able to master *all* forms or aspects of social activity, without the slightest exception (completing, after the conquest of political power, sometimes with great risk and tremendous danger, what had been left undone before this conquest); secondly, that the revolutionary classes must be ready for the most rapid and unexpected substitution of one form for another.

Everyone will agree that the behaviour of that army which does not prepare to master all types of weapons, all means and methods of warfare which the enemy may possess, is unwise and even criminal; but this applies even more to politics than to armies. In politics it is still less possible to foresee which means of struggle, under the varying future circumstances, will prove applicable and useful to us. If we do not possess all the means of struggle, we may suffer a heavy—at times even a decisive—defeat, if the changes in the situation of other classes which are beyond our control should make the order of the day that form of activity in which we are especially weak. Possessing all the means of struggle, we surely conquer, once we represent the interests of the truly foremost, truly revolutionary class, even though circumstances may not permit us to use all the weapons most dangerous to our enemy, weapons which the more quickly deal him deadly blows.

Inexperienced revolutionaries often think that legal means of struggle are opportunist, for the bourgeoisie often (especially in "peaceful" non-revolutionary times) use such legal means to deceive and fool the workers. On the other hand they think that illegal means in the struggle are revolutionary. This is not true. What is true is that the opportunists and traitors of the working class are those parties and leaders who are unable, or who do not want ("Don't say ' I can't,' say ' I won't ' ") to apply illegal means to the struggle. Take, for example, such conditions as prevailed during the imperialist war of 1914-1918, when the bourgeoisie of the freest democratic countries deceived the workers with an outrageous insolence and cruelty, prohibiting the truth as to the marauding character of the war to be spoken.

But those who cannot co-ordinate illegal forms of the struggle with legal ones are very poor revolutionaries. It is not at all difficult to be a good revolutionary once the revolution has already broken out—when all and every-one joins the revolution from mere enthusiasm, because it is the fashion, sometimes even from considerations of personal gain. It costs the proletariat labour, great labour and I may say excruciating pains, to rid itself after the victory of these pseudo-revolutionists. But it is far more difficult, and yet more valuable, to know how to be a revolutionary, even when conditions are yet lacking for direct, general, truly mass, and truly revolutionary action; to be able to defend the interests of the revolution by propaganda, agitation and organisation, in non-revolutionary institutions and often times in down-right reactionary surroundings, amongst masses that are incapable of imme-diately understanding the necessity for revolutionary methods. To be able to find, to sense, to determine the concrete plan of still incomplete revolu-tionary methods and measures, leading the masses to the real, decisive, final, great revolutionary struggle—this is the chief problem of modern Com-munism in Western Europe and America.

Take, for example, Britain. We cannot know, and no one is capable of predicting truly, how soon a real proletarian revolution will break out there, and what, more than any other, will be the cause which will awaken and inflame the now slumbering masses to revolution. It is therefore incumbent upon us to carry on our preparatory work so as to be "shod on all four feet," as the late Plekhanov was wont to say, when he was yet a Marxist and a revolutionist. Possibly it will be a parliamentary crisis which will "break the ice"; possibly it will be a crisis resulting from the hopelessly confused colonial and imperialist antagonisms, which become more and more painful and acute from day to day; possibly from some quite unseen third cause. We are not speaking of which struggle will decide the fate of the proletarian revolution in England—this question does not rouse any doubts in the minds of Communists, this question for all of us is decided and decided finally—we are speaking of what will induce the now slumbering prole-tarian masses to move towards and directly approach the revolution. Let us not forget how in the French bourgeois revolution, in a situation which, from the international and domestic aspect, was a hundred times less revolutionary than at present, such an unexpected and petty cause as one among thousands of dishonest tricks of the reactionary military caste (the Dreyfus case) was enough to bring the people face to face with civil war.

The Communists in Britain must continuously, assiduously and de-terminedly utilise both the parliamentary elections and every opening offered by the Irish, colonial and world-imperialist policy of the British Government, and all other aspects, domains and spheres of public life, working everywhere in the new Communist spirit the spirit not of the Second, but of the Third International. Neither time nor space permits me to describe here the manner of the Russian Bolshevik participation in the parliamentary elections and struggle; but I can assure the Communists abroad that it was not at all like the usual West European parliamentary campaign. From this the conclusion is often drawn "Oh, well, our parliamentarism is different from yours in Russia." This is the wrong conclusion. Communists, adherents to the Third International, exist in all countries precisely for the purpose of *adapting*, along the whole line, in every domain of life, the old Socialist, Trade Unionist, Syndicalist and parliamentarian activities to the new Communist idea. We, too, had plenty of opportunism, pure bourgeois traffickings, rascally capitalist dealings in our elections. The Communists of Western Europe and America must learn to create a new parliamentarism, entirely distinct from the usual opportunist, office-seeking form. This new parliamentarism must be used by the Communist Party to set forth its programme; it must be used by the real proletarian, who, in co-operation with the unorganised and very much ignored poor, should go from house to house of the workers, from hut to hut of the agricultural proletariat and isolated peasantry, carrying and distributing leaflets. (Fortunately, in Europe there are fewer isolated peasants than in Russia, and fewer still in England.) The Communist should penetrate into the humblest taverns, should find his way into the unions, societies, and chance gatherings of the common people and talk with them, not learnedly, nor too much after the parliamentary fashion. He should not for a moment think of a "place" in parliament; his only object should be everywhere to awaken the minds of the people, to attract the masses, to trip the bourgeoisie up on their own words, utilising the apparatus created by them, the election contests arranged by them, the appeals to the whole people issued by them, to preach Bolshevism to the masses. Under the rule of the bourgeoisie this is possible only during an election campaign—not counting, of course, the occasion of great strikes, when a similar apparatus of general agitation may be utilised, as we utilised it, still more intensely. It is exceedingly difficult to do this in Western Europe and America, but it can and must be done, for without labour the problems of Communism can in no way be solved. It is necessary to work for the solution of all *practical* problems which are becoming more and more varied, more and more involved with all branches of public life, as the Communists tend to conquer one field after another from the bourgeoisie.

Likewise in Britain it is necessary to put the work of propaganda, of agitation and organisation in the army, and among the nationalities oppressed and deprived of equal rights in "their" Empire (*e.g.*, Ireland, Egypt, etc.), on a new basis. This work must be carried on not on Socialist but on Communist lines, not in the reformist but in the revolutionary manner. For all these spheres of public life are especially filled with inflammable material and create many causes for conflicts, crises, enhancements of the class struggle. This is especially true in the epoch of imperialism generally, and particularly now when war has exhausted the peoples and has opened their eyes to the truth—namely, that tens of millions have been killed and maimed solely to decide whether English or German plunderers should rob more countries. We do not know, and we cannot know, which of the inflammable sparks which now fly in all countries, fanned by the economic and political world crisis, will be the one to start the conflagration (in the sense of a particular awakening of the masses); we are, therefore, bound to utilise our new Communist principles in the cultivation of all and every field of endeavour, no matter how old, rotten and seemingly hopeless. Otherwise we shall not be equal to the occasion, shall not be comprehensive, shall not be prepared to master all the types of weapons in the struggle, shall not be ready for victory over the bourgeoisie—which is responsible for the creation of all the aspects of public life, but which has now disrupted them, and disrupted them in a purely bourgeois manner. Not without careful preparation shall we be ready for the impending Communist reorganisation of society after our victory.

After the proletarian revolution in Russia and the victories (so unexpected for the bourgeoisie and all philistines) on an international scale of this revolution, the whole world has become different. The bourgeoisie, too, has changed. The bourgeoisie is scared and enraged by "Bolshevism," and has been driven almost to the point of madness. On the one hand it hastens the development of events, and on the other it concentrates its attention on the forcible suppression of Bolshevism, thus weakening its position in a great many other fields. The Communists of all advanced countries must reckon with both these circumstances in their tactics.

When the Russian Cadets (Constitutional Democrats) and Kerensky raised a hue-and-cry against the Bolsheviks (especially after April, 1917, and particularly in June-July, 1917), they rather "overdid it." Millions of copies of bourgeois papers, which were raising all sorts of howls against the Bolsheviks, helped to draw the masses into a study of Bolshevism; and, apart from the newspapers, the whole public, precisely because of the zeal of the bourgeoisie, was taken up with discussions about Bolshevism. At present, the millionaires of all countries are behaving, on an international scale, in such a manner as to deserve our heartiest thanks. They are hunting Bolshevism with the same zeal as did Kerensky and Co.; they are "overdoing it," and helping us quite as much as did Kerensky. When the French bourgeoisie makes Bolshevism the central point of the election campaign, scolding as Bolsheviks the comparatively moderate and vacillating Socialists; when the American bourgeoisie, having completely lost its head, seizes thousands and thousands of people upon suspicion of Bolshevism, and creates an atmosphere of panic, spreading alarms of Bolshevist plots broadcast; when the English bourgeoisie (the "sedatest" in the world), in spite of all its wisdom and experience, commits acts of incredible stupidity, forms the richest "Counter-Bolshevik" societies, creates a special literature on the subject, and hires for the struggle against it a large number of scientists, priests and agitators—we must then bow and thank these worthy capitalists. They work for us. They help us to get the masses interested in the question of the nature and significance of Bolshevism. And they cannot act otherwise; for to "pass over" Bolshevism in silence, to stifle it—in this they have already failed.

But at the same time the bourgeoisie sees in Bolshevism only one side— insurrection, violence, terror; it endeavours therefore to prepare itself especially for resistance and opposition in that direction alone. It is possible that in single cases, in individual countries, and for more or less short periods, it will succeed. We must reckon with such a possibility, and there is absolutely nothing dreadful to us in the fact that the bourgeoisie might have temporary success in this. Communism "springs up" from positively all sides of social life. Its sprouts are everywhere; the "contagion," to use the favourite and pleasant metaphor of the bourgeoisie and the bourgeois police, has very thoroughly penetrated the organism and totally impregnated it. If one of the outlets were to be stopped up with special care, the "contagion" would find another, sometimes a most unexpected, outlet. Life will assert itself. Leave the bourgeoisie to rage, let it work itself into a frenzy, commit stupidities, take vengeance in advance on the Bolsheviks, and endeavour to exterminate (in India, Hungary, Germany, etc.) more hundreds,

thousands, and hundreds of thousands of the Bolsheviks of yesterday and
to-morrow. Acting thus, the bourgeoisie acts as did all classes condemned to
death by history. Communists know that the future at any rate is theirs;
therefore, we can, and must, unite the intensest passion in the great revolutionary struggle with the coolest and soberest appreciation of the mad
ravings of the bourgeoisie. The Russian revolution was defeated heavily in
1905; the Russian Bolsheviks were beaten in July, 1917; over 15,000 German
Communists were killed by means of the clever provocation and the artful
manœuvres of Scheidemann and Noske, working with the bourgeoisie and
monarchist generals; White Terror is raging in Finland and Hungary. But
in all cases and in all countries Communism grows and is hardened; its roots
are so deep that persecution neither weakens nor debilitates, but rather
strengthens it. Only one thing more is needed to lead us surely and firmly to
victory, namely, the consciousness everywhere that all Communists, in all
countries, must display a maximum *flexibility* in their tactics. The only
thing wanting to Communism, which is splendidly advancing, especially
in the advanced countries, is this consciousness and the skill of applying it in
practice.

That which has happened to Kautsky, Otto Bauer and others, highly
erudite Marxists, devoted to Socialism, and leaders of the Second International, could and ought to serve as a useful lesson. They fully appreciated
the necessity of pliable tactics, they learned and taught to others the Marxist
dialectics—and much of what they have done in that respect will remain for
ever a valuable acquisition to Socialist literature. But in the application of
these dialectics they made a great mistake; they showed themselves in
practice to be so *un*dialectic, and so incapable of reckoning with the rapid
changes of forms and the rapid filling of old forms with new contents, that
their fate is not much more enviable than that of Hyndman, Guesde and
Plekhanov. The main reason for their bankruptcy was that their eyes were
"fastened" upon one fixed form of the growth of the working-class movement
and of Socialism. They forgot all about its one-sidedness, and were afraid
to perceive the sharp break which, by virtue of objective conditions, became
unavoidable; so they continue to repeat the simple, at first glance self-
evident truth, once learned by rote; "Three are more than two." But
politics resembles algebra more than arithmetic, and it is more like higher
than lower mathematics. In reality all the old forms of the Socialist movement have been filled with new contents; there appears before the figures,

consequently, a new sign, a "minus"; and our wiseacres stubbornly continue to persuade themselves and others that "minus three" is more than "minus two"!

Communists must endeavour not to repeat the same mistake; or, to speak more percisely, the same mistake—committed the other way round by the Left Communists—must be corrected sooner and more quickly in order to get rid of it with less pain to the organism. Not only Right but Left doctrinairism is a mistake. Of course the mistake of the latter in Communism is at the present moment a thousand times less dangerous and less significant than the mistake of Right doctrinairism (*i.e.*, social-chauvinism and Kautskianism); but, after all, this is due to the fact that Left Communism is quite a young current, just coming into being. For this reason the disease under certain conditions can be easily cured, and it is necessary to begin its treatment with the utmost energy.

The old forms have burst; for the contents (anti-proletarian and re-actionary) obtained an inordinate development. We now have, from the standpoint of the development of international Communism, strong, power-ful contents at work for Soviet power and the proletarian dictatorship, and these can and must manifest themselves in any form, new as old; the new spirit can and must regenerate, conquer and subjugate all forms, not only the new but the old, not for the purpose of reconciling the new with the old forms, but to enable us to forge all forms, new and old, into a weapon for the final decisive and unswerving victory of Communism.

The Communists must strain every effort to direct the movement of the working class, and the development of society generally, along the straightest and quickest way to the universal victory of Soviet power and the prole-tarian dictatorship. This truth is incontestable. But it is enough to take one little step farther—a step it would seem in the same direction—and truth is transformed into error! It is enough to say, as do the German and British "Left" Communists, that we acknowledge only one straight road, that we do not admit manœuvres, co-operation, compromises—and this will already be a mistake, which is capable of bringing, and, in fact, has brought and is bringing, the most serious harm to Communism. Right doctrinairism has foundered on the recognition of only the old forms, and has become totally bankrupt, not having perceived the new contents. Left doctrinairism un-conditionally repudiates certain old forms, failing to see that the new con-tent is breaking its way through all and every form, that it is our duty as

Communists to master them all, to learn how to supplement, with the maximum rapidity, one form by another, and to adapt our tactics to all such changes, caused not by our class nor by our endeavours.

World revolution has been given a powerful impetus by the horrors, atrocities and villainies of the world imperialist war, and by the hopelessness of the position created by it. This revolution is spreading more widely and deeply with such supreme rapidity, with such splendid richness of varying forms, with such an instructive, practical refutation of all doctrinairism, that there is every hope of a speedy and thorough recovery of the international Communist movement from the infantile disorder of "Left" Communism.

April 27, 1920.

Appendix

¶ *While the problem of publishing this brochure was being solved in our country—robbed as she was by the imperialists of the whole world, who are wreaking vengeance upon her because of the proletarian revolution, and who continued to rob and blockade her in spite of promises to their own workers—there came from abroad additional material. Not pretending to make in my brochure more than the general remarks of a publicist, I shall only briefly touch upon some points.*

I

The Split of the German Communist Party.

THE split of the German Communists has become an accomplished fact. The "Left" or "Opposition in principle" has established a separate "Communist Labour Party" in contradistinction to the "Communist Party." There is evidence that Italy is also approaching a similar split. I make this statement subject to correction, as I only possess the additional numbers—numbers 7 and 8—of the "Left" paper, *Il Soviet,* which openly deals with the possibility and the inevitably of a split. There are also discussions concerning a forthcoming conference of the "Abstentionist" group (in other words, of the group of boycottists or opponents of participation in Parliament) a group that was, hitherto, part of the Italian Socialist Party.

There is reason to apprehend that the split with the "Left" anti-parliamentarians, and partly also with the anti-politicals (who are in opposition to the political parties and Trade Union activity), will become an international phenomenon, similar to the split with the "Centrists" (*i.e.,* Kautskians, the Longuetists, the Independents, and so forth.) Be it so. A split is, at all events, preferable to a muddle, which is a hindrance both to ideological, theoretical and revolutionary growth; a hindrance to the maturing of the party and to its organised work of practical preparation for the dictatorship of the proletariat.

Let the "Left" make an attempt to prepare (and then to realise) on a national and international scale, the dictatorship of the proletariat; let them attempt to do this without a strictly centralised, disciplined, party, capable of leading and managing every branch, every sphere, every variety of political and cultural work. Practical experience will soon make them wiser.

Every effort must be made in order that the split with the "Left" shall impede or hinder as little as possible the amalgamation into one common party—inevitable in the near future—of all participators in the Labour Movement who are sincerely and whole-heartedly in favour of the Soviet system and proletarian dictatorship. It was a peculiar stroke of luck for the Russian Bolsheviks that they had fifteen years of systematic and decisive fighting, both against the Mensheviks (that is to say, the opportunists and "Centrists") as well as against the "Left," long before the direct mass struggle for proletarian dictatorship. The same work has to be performed now in

Europe and in America by means of "forced marches." It may happen that individual personalities, especially those belonging to the category of unsuccessful pretenders to leadership, will, through the lack of proletarian discipline and "intellectual honesty," adhere for a long time to their mistakes. As far as the working masses are concerned, when the moment arrives they will amalgamate naturally, and unite all sincere Communists under a common banner into a common party, capable of realising the Soviet system and the dictatorship of the proletariat.*

---

* I shall make the following remark with regard to the question of the future amalgamation of the "Left" Communists (anti-parliamentarians) and Communists generally. As far as I can judge by the acquaintance I have formed of the newspapers of the "Left", and those of the German Communists in general, the first have the advantage over the second in that they are better agitators among the masses. I have repeatedly observed something analogous in the history of the Bolshevik Party—though on a smaller scale, and in individual local organisations, never on a national scale. For instance, in 1907-1908 the "Left" Bolsheviks had, upon certain occasions and in many places, better success in propaganda among the masses than we had. In a revolutionary moment, or at a time when revolutionary recollections are still fresh, it is most easy to approach the masses with the tactics of mere negation. This, however, can hardly serve as an argument for the correctness of such tactics. At all events, there is not the least doubt that the Communist Party, which actually wishes to be the advance guard of the revolutionary class of the proletariat, and which, in addition wishes to lead the general masses (not only the wide proletarian masses, but also the non-proletarian toilers and exploited), must necessarily be capable of propaganda, of organisation, and of agitation in the most accessible, most comprehensible form ; must demonstrate clearly and graphically, not only for the town and factory man-in-the-street, but also for the whole of the village population.

2

Communists and Independents in Germany.

IN my brochure I have ventured an opinion to the effect that a compromise between the Communists and the "Left" wing of the Independents is necessary and useful to Communism, but that it will be difficult to effect this. The newspapers which I have subsequently received have confirmed both aspects of my opinion. A "statement" of the Central Committee of the German Communist Party on the military outburst of Kapp-Luttwitz and on the "Socialist Government" has been published in No. 32 of the *Red Banner* (*Die Rote Fahne*, the organ of the Communist Party of Germany March 26, 1920.) From the point of view both of basic principle and of practical conclusions, this statement is perfectly correct. Its basic position is that an objective basis is lacking at the present moment for proletarian dictatorship, in view of the fact that the majority of the town workers are in favour of the Independents. The conclusion arrived at was: the promise of a "loyal opposition" to the Government, that is to say, a repudiation of an armed coup d'état, provided that this be "a Socialist Government excluding all capitalist and bourgeois parties."

Undoubtedly this was correct tactics. But, if it is hardly worth while to dwell on trifling inexactitudes, yet it is difficult to pass over in silence such a glaring misunderstanding as the one caused by the official statement of the Communist Party; the government of social traitors is called "Socialist"; it is hardly possible to speak of "the exclusion of bourgeois-capitalist parties" when the parties of both Scheidemann and Messrs. Kautsky-Crispien are petit-bourgeois-democratic; it is hardly permissible to write such things as those contained in paragraph 4 of the declaration, which is to the following effect:—

> In order further to gain the sympathy of the proletarian masses in favour of Communism, a state of things under which political freedom can be fully utilised and under which bourgeois democracy could in no case manifest itself as a dictatorship of capital—such a state of things is of great importance from the point of view of the development of proletarian dictatorship. . . .

Such a state of things is an impossibility. Petit bourgeois leaders, the German Hendersons and Snowdens (Scheidemann and Crispien) cannot possibly abandon bourgeois democracy, which in its turn cannot but be a capitalist dictatorship. From the point of view of the attainment of practical results, as correctly pursued by the Central Committee of the Party, there was no necessity at all to write such a statement, incorrect in principle and politically harmful. If one wishes to indulge in parliamentary language, it is sufficient to say "So long as the majority of the town workers follow the Independents, we Communists cannot possibly interfere with the workers in their desire to live out their last illusions of middle-class democracy (consequently, also bourgeois-capitalist illusions) in practical experience with their own governments." This is sufficient for the justification of the compromise, for which there is a real necessity, and which means that, for a certain period, all attempts at a violent overthrow of the government which enjoys the confidence of a majority of the town workers must be abandoned. In every-day mass agitation, unconnected with any form of officialdom or Parliamentary politeness, it is, of course, quite possible to add: "Let such knaves and fools as the Scheidemanns and the Kautsky-Crispiens actually reveal the full extent to which they are themselves deceived and to which they deceive the workers; their 'pure' government will itself make the 'cleanest' possible sweep of the Augean stables of Socialism, Social Democracy and all other forms of social treason."

There is no foundation for the statement that the present leaders of the German Independent Social-Democratic Party have lost all influence; in reality, they are more dangerous to the proletariat than the Hungarian Social Democrats, who styled themselves Communists and promised to "support" the dictatorship of the proletariat. The real nature of these leaders has asserted itself repeatedly during the German Kornilov period—*i.e.,* during the Luttwitz-Kapp coup d'état. The short articles of Karl Kautsky serve as a miniature, but vivid, example. These are entitled "Decisive Moments" and appear in the *Freiheit,* the organ of the Independents (March 30, 1920). There is also the article by Arthur Crispien entitled "The Political Situation" (ibid April 14, 1920). These men are absolutely incapable of thinking and reasoning like revolutionaries. They are sentimental middle-class democrats, who are a thousand times more dangerous to the proletariat when they proclaim themselves to be adherents of the Soviet system and of proletarian dictatorship; for, as a matter of course, they will, upon every critical and difficult occasion, commit acts of treason—"sincerely" confident all the time that they are assisting the proletariat! Is it not a fact that, when the Hungarian Social-Democrats quailed and whined before the agents of the Entente capitalists and the Entente executioners, they claimed that all the time their one desire was to "assist" the proletariat! And these were men who had undergone a Communist baptism, but who, owing to their cowardice and lack of character, considered the position of the Soviet Government in Hungary as hopeless.

3

Turati & Co. in Italy.

THE copies of the Italian newspaper *Il Soviet,* referred to above, fully confirm all that I have said in my brochure regarding the error of the Italian Socialist Party, which suffers in its ranks such members and groups of Parliamentarians. It is still better confirmed by a layman, in the person of the Rome correspondent of the British bourgeois Liberal newspaper, the *Manchester Guardian,* whose interview with Turati is published in that paper on March 12, 1920.

Signor Turati, writes this correspondent, is of opinion that the revolutionary peril is not such as to cause undue anxiety in Italy. The Maximalists are fanning the flame of Soviet theories only to keep the masses awake and excited. These theories are, however, merely legendary notions, unripe programmes, incapable of being put to practical use. They are useful only to maintain the working classes in a state of expectation. The very men who employ them as a lure to dazzle proletarian eyes find themselves frequently compelled to fight a daily battle for the extortion of some trifling economic advantages, so as to delay the moment when the working class will lose their illusions and faith in their favourite myths. Hence a long string of strikes of all sizes and with all pretexts, up to the very latest ones in the mail and railway services—which make the already hard conditions of the country still worse. The country is irritated owing to the difficulties connected with its Adriatic problem, it is weighed down by its foreign debt and by its inflated paper circulation, and yet it is far from realising the necessity of adopting that discipline of work which alone can restore order and prosperity.

It is as clear as daylight that the English correspondent has let slip the truth —which in all probability is partly concealed and improved upon by Turati himself, his bourgeois defenders, assistants, and inspirers in Italy. The truth in question is to the effect that the ideas and the political activity of such men as Turati, Treves, Modigliani, Dugoni and Co. is actually and precisely such as that described by the British correspondent. It is social-treachery, pure and simple. It is so symptomatic, this defence of "order and discipline" for workers who are wage slaves, for workers who toil to enrich the capitalists. And how well we Russians are acquainted with all these Menshevik speeches!

How valuable this recognition that the masses are in favour of the Soviet form of government! This inability to conceive the revolutionary importance of the strike wave, growing irrepressibly, how stupid and how meanly middle-class it is! Yes, yes, the British correspondent of the bourgeois Liberal paper has rendered an ill service to Messrs. Turati and Co., and has well confirmed the just demands of Comrade Bordiga and his friends of *Il Soviet,* who are insisting that the Italian Socialist Party, if its intention to go with the Third International be real, should expel from its ranks with all the ignominy they deserve Messrs Turati and Co., and should become a Communist Party not only in word but in deed.

4

Incorrect Conclusions drawn from Correct Premises.

YET Comrade Bordiga and his "Left" friends draw from their correct criticism of Messrs. Turati and Co. the wrong conclusion that Parliamentary participation is harmful generally. The Italian "Left" are incapable of bringing forward even a shadow of serious argument in support of this view.   They do not know (or they are trying to forget), the international instances of actual revolutionary and Communist utilisation of the bourgeois parliaments—a utilisation which is essential for the proletarian revolution. They simply fail to conceive the new tactics and, repeating themselves endlessly, they keep up the cry regarding the old non-Bolshevik utilisation of parliamentarism.

This is their cardinal mistake. Communism must introduce its new method, not only into parliament, but in every sphere of activity. The aim of this new method is, whilst retaining and developing all that is good in the Second International, radically to break with the traditions of that International; but without long and persistent labour this cannot be effected.

As an instance, let us take the Press. Newspapers, brochures, proclamations fulfil a necessary work of propaganda, agitation, and organisation. Without a journalistic apparatus, no single mass movement can go on in a more or less civilised country. And, to carry on the work of the Press, it is absolutely necessary to employ the services of men from the bourgeois-intellectual class. No outcry against leaders, no kind of pledge or promise to preserve the purity of the masses from their influence, can abolish this necessity, can abolish the bourgeois democratic setting and atmosphere of property in which this work is being carried on under capitalism. Even two and a-half years after the overthrow of the bourgeoisie and the acquirement of political power by the proletariat, we still see around us this atmosphere of mass (peasant and craftsman), bourgeois-democratic, property relations.

Parliamentarism is one form of activity, journalism is another. Both can be Communist and should be Communist, when the active workers in either sphere are really Communists, are really members of the proletarian mass party. Yet in one as well as in the other (and, for the matter of that, in *any* sphere of activity), under the system of capitalism and during the transition period from capitalism to Socialism, it is impossible to avoid those difficulties which are inherent in their present organisation. It is for the proletariat to solve the problem of utilising for its own ends its assistants, press or political, of a bourgeois turn of mind; of gaining a victory over the bourgeois intellectual prejudices and influences; of weakening and, ultimately, of completing the transformation of the petit-bourgeois atmosphere.

Have we not all been witnesses of an abundance of instances, in all countries prior to the war of 1914–1918, of extreme "Left" Anarchists, Syndicalists and others denouncing parliamentarism, and deriding parliamentary Socialists who became middle-class, flaying them as place-seekers and so forth, and yet themselves making the same kind of bourgeois career through the Press and through syndicalist trade union activity? To quote only France, are not the examples of Messrs. Jouhaux and Merrheim typical enough?

That is why the "repudiation" of participation in Parliament is mere childishness. Those who would boycott Parliament think it possible to "solve," by such a "simple" and "easy," alleged revolutionary, method, the difficult problem of the struggle against bourgeois democratic influences *within* the labour movement. In reality they are fleeing from their own shadow, they are closing their eyes to difficulties, and satisfying themselves with mere words. And there is no doubt whatever that capitalism universally generates, not only outside the labour movement, but also within it, certain prevailing characteristic traits, such as shameless place-hunting, a bourgeois readiness to accept soft jobs in the Government, a glaring reformist corruption in parliamentary activity, despicable middle-class routine. But this capitalist and bourgeois atmosphere disappears but slowly even after the overthrow of the bourgeoisie (owing to the fact that the latter is constantly reborn from the peasantry), and the same atmosphere tends to permeate every sphere of activity and life, still reappearing in the form of place-hunting, national chauvinism and middle-classness of outlook and attitude, etc.

To yourselves, dear boycottists and anti-parliamentarians, you seem to be "terribly revolutionary," but in reality you are intimidated by comparatively small difficulties in the struggle against bourgeois influences within the labour movement, when actually your victory—*i.e.*, the overthrow of the bourgeoisie and the conquest of the political power by the proletariat, will create these very difficulties on an infinitely larger scale. Like children, you have become frightened of a difficulty which confronts you to-day, failing to understand that, to-morrow and the day after, you will have to learn to overcome the same kind of difficulties, but on a far larger scale.

Under the Soviet form of government, both our and your parties are invaded by an ever-growing number of bourgeois intellectuals. They will find their way into the Soviets, and into the courts of law, and into every sphere of administration, as it is impossible to build up Communism otherwise than out of the human material created by capitalism. Since it is impossible to expel and to destroy the bourgeois intelligentsia, it becomes indispensable to conquer this intelligentsia, to change, to re-train and to re-educate it, just as it is necessary to re-educate, in the process of a long struggle, the proletariat itself, on the basis of proletarian dictatorship. The proletariat cannot abolish its own petit-bourgeois prejudices at one miraculous stroke; this can be accomplished neither by the command of the Virgin Mary, nor by any slogan, resolution, or decree, but only by dint of a long and difficult mass struggle against petit-bourgeois influence. The same problems which at the present time the anti-parliamentarians brush aside with one hand so proudly, so loftily, so lightly, so childishly, will, under the Soviet system of government, arise *within* the very Soviets themselves, within the Soviet administration, with the Soviet "legal defenders." We have done well to abolish in Russia the bourgeois law fraternity, but it is reviving here under the cover of Soviet "legal defenders." In the case of the Soviet engineers, the Soviet teachers, and the privileged (*i.e.*, the better skilled and better paid) working men at the Soviet factories, we observe a constant revival of absolutely all the negative traits peculiar to the bourgeois parliamentarism. It is only by dint of a constant, untiring, long and stubborn struggle of proletarian organisation and discipline that we can gradually conquer this evil.

True enough, under bourgeois domination it is most "difficult" to conquer bourgeois habits in one's own party—*i.e.*, the labour party; it is "difficult" to expel from the party the accustomed parliamentary leaders who are hopelessly corrupt with bourgeois prejudices; it is "difficult" to subject the absolutely necessary, even if limited, number, of bourgeois intellectuals to proletarian discipline; it is "difficult" to form, in the bourgeois parliament, a Communist Group worthy of the working class; it is "difficult" to ensure that the Communist parliamentarians do not engage in the bourgeois parliamentary game of wire-pulling, but take up the necessary and actual work of agitation, propaganda and organisation of the masses. All this is most "difficult," there is no doubt about it; it was a difficult thing in Russia, and it is a still more difficult thing in Western Europe and in America, where the bourgeoisie is far stronger, and where bourgeois democratic traditions, and so forth, are more hide-bound.

Yet all these "difficulties" are playthings in comparison with the *same kind* of problems with which the proletariat will inevitably be confronted just the same, and which it will be obliged to solve for the sake of its victory, both during the revolution and after the conquest of power by the proletariat. During the period of proletarian dictatorship it will become necessary to re-educate millions of peasants and small-owners of property, hundreds of thousands of employees, of officials, and of bourgeois intellectuals; it will become necessary to subject them all to the proletarian State and to proletarian leadership, to suppress and conquer in them their bourgeois habits and traditions. In comparison with these truly gigantic problems, it becomes a childishly easy matter to establish, under the bourgeois dictatorship and in the bourgeois parliament, a real Communist Group of a real proletarian party.

If our "Left" comrades and anti-parliamentarians fail now to learn to overcome even such small difficulties, we may assert with confidence that they will prove incapable of realising proletarian dictatorship, of dealing on a large scale with the problem of changing the bourgeois intellectuals and the bourgeois institutions. Alternatively, they will have to complete their education in a hurry; and this haste will render great harm to the cause of the proletariat, and will cause it to commit more errors than usual, and to manifest more weakness and inefficiency than usual.

So long as the bourgeoisie is not overthrown, and, subsequently, until small economy and small production have utterly disappeared—the bourgeois atmosphere, proprietary habits, middle-class traditions, will impair the proletarian work from without as well as from within the labour movement; not only in the one sphere of parliamentary activity, but unavoidably in each and every sphere of social activity, in each and in every branch of politics, culture and life, this bourgeois atmosphere will manifest itself. The attempt to brush aside, to do away with, *one* of the "unpleasant" problems or difficulties in one field of activity, is a profound mistake and one which will have to be paid for dearly. It is necessary to learn and to master every sphere of activity and work without exception, to overcome all difficulties and all bourgeois habits, customs, and traditions. To put the question in any other form is to refuse to treat it seriously, and is mere childishness.

May 12, 1920.

5

IN the Russian text of this book, I in some degree misrepresented the conduct of the Dutch Communist Party, as a whole, in international revolutionary politics. I therefore take this opportunity to publish the letter, given below, of the Dutch comrades on this point, and, further, to correct the expression "Dutch Tribunists," which I used in the Russian version, and to substitute for it "some members of the Dutch Communist Party."

N. LENIN

A Letter from Wijnkoop.

Moscow,
June 30, 1920.

DEAR COMRADE LENIN,—

THANKS to your kindness we, the members of the Dutch Delegation to the Second Congress of the Communist International, could look over your book, *"Left Wing" Communism: An Infantile Disorder,* before the translations into the Western European languages were published.

In this book of yours, you emphasise several times your disapproval of the rôle some of the members of the Dutch Communist Party have played in international politics.

We, however, must protest against your making the Communist Party responsible for their deeds. It is utterly incorrect. Moreover, it is unjust. For these members of the Dutch Communist Party hardly, or not at all, participated in the every-day fight of our party; also, directly or indirectly, they are trying to introduce oppositional slogans in the Communist Party, against which the Dutch Party, and everyone of its organs, with all their energy, have fought and are fighting, up till to-day.

Fraternally yours,
(*For the Dutch Delegation*)
D. J. WIJNKOOP

9 781684 222179